# SJWs
## ALWAYS LIE

CASTALIA HOUSE

### NON-FICTION
*Astronomy and Astrophysics* by Dr. Sarah Salviander
*A History of Strategy: From Sun Tzu to William S. Lind* by Martin van Creveld
*Equality: The Impossible Quest* by Martin van Creveld
*On War: The Collected Columns of William S. Lind 2003-2009* by William S. Lind
*Four Generations of Modern War* by William S. Lind
*Transhuman and Subhuman: Essays on Science Fiction and Awful Truth* by John C.
    Wright
*SJWs Always Lie: Taking Down the Thought Police* by Vox Day

### MILITARY SCIENCE FICTION
*Riding the Red Horse Vol. 1* ed. Tom Kratman and Vox Day
*There Will Be War Vol. I* ed. Jerry Pournelle
*There Will Be War Vol. II* ed. Jerry Pournelle

### SCIENCE FICTION
*Awake in the Night* by John C. Wright
*Awake in the Night Land* by John C. Wright
*City Beyond Time: Tales of the Fall of Metachronopolis* by John C. Wright
*Somewhither* by John C. Wright
*Big Boys Don't Cry* by Tom Kratman
*The Stars Came Back* by Rolf Nelson
*Hyperspace Demons* by Jonathan Moeller
*On a Starry Night* by Tedd Roberts
*Do Buddhas Dream of Enlightened Sheep* by Josh M. Young
*QUANTUM MORTIS A Man Disrupted* by Steve Rzasa and Vox Day
*QUANTUM MORTIS A Mind Programmed* by Jeff Sutton, Jean Sutton, and Vox Day
*Victoria: A Novel of Fourth Generation War* by Thomas Hobbes

### FANTASY
*One Bright Star to Guide Them* by John C. Wright
*The Book of Feasts & Seasons* by John C. Wright
*A Throne of Bones* by Vox Day
*Summa Elvetica: A Casuistry of the Elvish Controversy* by Vox Day

### CASTALIA CLASSICS
*The Programmed Man* by Jean and Jeff Sutton
*Apollo at Go* by Jeff Sutton
*First on the Moon* by Jeff Sutton

# VOX DAY

# SJWs

## ALWAYS LIE

Taking Down the Thought Police

SJWs Always Lie: Taking Down the Thought Police

by Vox Day

Published by Castalia House
Kouvola, Finland
www.castaliahouse.com

Cover Design: JartStar
Foreword: Milo Yiannopoulos
Interior Cartoons: Red Meat

# Contents

# PRAISE FOR VOX DAY

*"Vox Day is one sick puppy."*

—Dr. P.Z. Myers, PhD

*"Vox Day is a fascist mega-dickbag and less a human being than one long sequence of junk* DNA.*"*

—Dr. Phil Sandifer, PhD

*"I consider Vox Day one step, either direction, from certifiable."*

—Mike Resnick, science fiction author, 38-time
Hugo Award nominee

*"I think I have made my disgust with Vox Day and his Rabid Puppies clear."*

—George R. R. Martin, fantasy author, 19-time
Hugo Award nominee

*"Vox Day rises all the way to 'downright evil'."*

—Patrick Nielsen Hayden, Manager of Science Fiction, Tor Books,
15-time Hugo Award nominee

*"Vox Day is a real bigoted shithole of a human being."*

—John Scalzi, three-time SFWA President and science fiction author,
9-time Hugo nominee

*"Vox Day and his followers made it impossible for me to remain silent, keep calm, and carry on."*

—Connie Willis, science fiction author, 24-time
Hugo Award nominee

*"Vox Day set out to hurt the* SF *genre by damaging our award system."*

—David Gerrold, science fiction author, 4-time
Hugo Award nominee

*"The real burning question is, 'what will Vox Day attack next?'"*

—Charles Stross, science fiction author, 15-time
Hugo Award nominee

# DEDICATION

This book is for all the gamers around the world who simply wanted to be left alone to play their games in peace. You didn't go looking to fight a cultural war, the social justice warriors in game journalism brought their war to you.

This book is for Adam Baldwin and Internet Aristocrat, for Sargon of Akkad and RogueStar and The Ralph Retort, for Ultra (who exposed the GameJournoPros), for Draginol and Grummz and all the devs of GG, for Christina Hoff Summers and Mercedes Carrera, for Yuji Nakajima and Oliver Campbell and Kukuruyo, for A Girl in Vermillion and A Mage in Black and MegaSpacePanda, for Doctor Ethics and Alejandro Argandona and Thurin and my man Daddy Warpig, for Paolo Munoz and Deep Freeze and Otter Jesus, for Shauna and Spacebunny, for Allum Bokhari and Mike Cernovich, and, of course, for the literally indefatigable Milo Yiannopoulos.

We'll always have Paris, Milo.

This book is for the thousands of sealions whose names I don't know, who sent emails and created memes, who persisted and leveled up, and who, in doing so, shattered the SJW Narrative.

This book is for #GAMERGATE.

# FOREWORD

Social justice divides the world into good and evil. It is a starkly Manichean view of the moral universe: one that pits heroic LGBT campaigners, feminists, transgender activists and #BLACKLIVESMATTER protesters against the jackbooted fascists of the patriarchal, capitalist Establishment.

Yet dig a little deeper, and you realise that the social justice view of the world is horribly patronising, two-dimensional and depressing. It suggests that our aspirations and opinions are necessarily bound by our circumstances of birth: that homosexuals must support grotesquely engorged public sectors to pay for "homophobia awareness" organisations whether they are needed or not; that women are always and in every circumstance victims; that blacks cannot succeed in life without special treatment.

This tendency never survives contact with reality because it never sees the exceptions coming. Social justice warriors don't understand that life, and people, are messy and complicated: that a gay person might, for entirely rational reasons and without a shred of self-loathing, object to the idea of gay marriage.

*SJWs Always Lie* is a truism because you cannot make social justice arguments without purposefully omitting crucial facts. You cannot, in other words, be a social justice warrior in good faith.

SJWs see no irony in judging people according to their orientation, skin colour and gender, particularly if they are "straight", "white" and "male."

But even those of us on the fringes struggle to escape censure. I was born a conservative, but I chose to be homosexual. According to the most fashionable thinking in American media and the academy, I should not exist.

The fact that I am gay yet refuse to acquiesce to third-wave feminism or grievance politics of any other kind strikes my ideological opponents as one of the great unexplained mysteries of the universe. (It's why they can't beat me in television debates.) Believing that a person's sex, race and orientation defines the acceptable limits of the opinions they may hold is called "identity politics." It's a bizarre but flourishing cult in America today that makes fools of its supporters by presenting an insultingly reductionist view of human nature.

We're familiar with the attitude from stereotypical, sadistic preachers of popular fiction, but not for a hundred years here in the West have so many people from so many pedestals insisted on dictating to the rest of us how we shall live.

From the dishonest critics of GamerGate to the bigoted and insulting #KillAllMen and #GiveYourMoneyToWomen hashtags, the social justice tendency is a narrow, bossy and often prurient prism from which to view humanity, and one that has acquired, as this book ably demonstrates, an especially poisonous self-righteousness in the last few years.

Of course, authoritarians are not restricted to one side of the political divide. Nevertheless, it is an ironic and remarkable feature of the American Left that there is no longer space for liberals within American liberalism. That will be a disaster for Left-wing politicians and thinkers in future years because the great battle of the next decade won't be between left- and right-wing visions of how society ought to be organised, but between the control freaks at *Vice* and *Buzzfeed* and the classical liberals of reddit, Twitter and the various image boards. The Left will be relegated to spectator status while the conflict plays out.

Thanks to the intellectual fragility of social justice, its adherents have become rightly notorious for their cruel, hysterical and sociopathic modus operandi. But while the public is turning its back on lunatics in new media who claim that how men sit on the subway expresses something profound about the relationship between men and women, the zealots still occupy positions of influence in our society.

Fortunately, there is a powerful weapon in our arsenal against the hand-wringers, pearl-clutchers, guilt-mongers and professional panickers—ridicule. You don't have to agree with everything Vox Day writes on his popular blog to recognise that he is a master of the art of needling social justice warriors and one of the loudest and most persistent voices of the resistance. For writing this book he deserves our thanks.

*Milo Yiannopoulos*
*Miami, Florida*
*August 2015*

# PROLOGUE

*Social justice does not belong to the category of error but to that of nonsense, like the term 'a moral stone'.*

—F.A. Hayek, *Law, Legislation and Liberty, Volume 2: The Mirage of Social Justice*, 1976

One cannot truly understand the depths of total dishonesty to which Social Justice Warriors are willing to descend until one has experienced being a direct target of their unrestrained use of the politics of personal destruction.

In December 2012, I announced my candidacy for the presidency of SFWA, the Science Fiction and Fantasy Writers Association, because it seemed obvious to me at the time that the organization was hopelessly out of date after years of being run by amateurs. Here was a *science fiction* association that in the second decade of the 21st century still snail-mailed a print publication to its members. It was an organization that couldn't even get its own acronym right. And even though self-published writers were already selling tens of millions of ebooks on Amazon, and many of them were actually outselling most of the Active and Associate members of SFWA, a writer couldn't join the association unless he'd published three short stories in the increasingly small number of approved publications or published a novel with one of the approved publishers.

Their own legal adviser repeatedly commented on how insane it was that the association farmed out the responsibility for deciding who could become a member or not to the very publishers whose interests SFWA had been founded to oppose.

In addition to those idiosyncracies, the previous administration had been dumb enough to publicly take on Amazon, then Random House, which was rather like a one-winged mosquito announcing to the world that it was going to drain an elephant dry before sucking all the blood out of a hippopotamus. My fellow members also had a disturbingly snobbish tendency to sneer at media tie-in books despite the fact that four of the ten best-selling novels published by the largest science fiction publisher, Tor Books, were *Star Wars* and *Halo* tie-in novels.

So, being a professional game designer and a published fantasy novelist who had been a Life Member of the organization for more than a decade, I thought I might be able to help SFWA come to terms with the post-Gutenberg world of ebooks, smartphones, and virtual goods that had so many of its members reeling in confusion and disarray. Furthermore, unlike most of its past presidents, I had a fair amount of corporate executive experience. I even thought that due to my personal connections to various executives at tech companies like Amazon and Google, I might be able to help the association avoid some of the clumsier PR debacles it was in the habit of creating for itself. And while I wasn't popular in certain SF circles due to my having previously been a nationally syndicated opinion writer for Universal Press Syndicate, SFWA was an apolitical professional authors association, right?

I could not have been more wrong.

I posted my candidacy on the members-only SFWA Forum along with my presidential platform. I hadn't been particularly active in the organization over the years, but I did serve on three Nebula Award juries without incident, so this wasn't the first time I'd gotten involved in some capacity. Here are a few of the ideas I put forth in my 12-point platform, none of which had anything whatsoever to do with politics or ideology.

- SPLIT THE NEBULA AWARDS: Science fiction is not fantasy. Fantasy is not science fiction. I propose doubling the number of Nebula Awards and presenting awards for Best Novel, Best Novella, Best Novelette, Best Short Story, and Best Script in two categories, Science Fiction and Fantasy.

- AWARD A CASH PRIZE FOR BOTH BEST NOVEL AWARDS: A $5,000 prize will be awarded to the winner of Best Novel: Science Fiction as well as to the winner of Best Novel: Fantasy. The long term goal will be to work towards making the winning of a Nebula a more prestigious and financially valuable event than winning the Man Booker Prize.

- EXPAND THE MEMBERSHIP: The right to SFWA membership will be granted to all self-published and small press-published authors who have sold more than a specified number of ebooks to be determined, eligibility number to be confirmed via official Amazon report. It will also be granted to all SF/F-related computer game lead designers, senior designers, and writers with primary credits on two or more SF/F-related games.

- ELIMINATE THE APPEARANCE OF CORRUPTION IN THE AWARD PROCESS: Closing the nomination process to the membership and the public made the appearance of corruption worse, not better. Reducing the number of recommendations to reduce logrolling was a good idea; hiding the results from the membership created more harm than good.

Much to my surprise, very few of the association's members were even remotely interested in discussing these or any of the other new ideas I'd put forward. Instead, I was subjected to amateur ad-hoc psychoanalysis, asked a series of increasingly bizarre and irrelevant questions, and forced to put up with nonsensical grandstanding by those who opposed my candidacy. Con-

sider just a few of the strange statements made by the members when given
the opportunity to ask questions of the candidates.

- Are there examples in your personal history where you worked for
  others without any gain for yourself?

- I've seen your blogs, and as a woman I am BEYOND offended by them.
  If, by some weird fluke you were to win the election, I would immediately resign from the organization. In fact, I'm more than a little
  appalled and disgusted that you are a member of it, and as such have
  access to my address and phone number. What can you say to change
  my mind?

- It seems to me that your obvious contempt for women writers, should
  you be elected, will redefine the nature of the organization in a
  way that models your ideology—an ideology which entirely devalues
  women writers, not to mention a great percentage of certain kinds of
  writing within the genre. So your public statements concerning publishing and writing and women indicate that you cannot represent a
  significant portion of the membership. Because you simply do not
  value those writers, you will be unable to do those things that would
  support our careers.

- As much as one might think that your preferences don't apply, your
  personal views do inform your position and platform, though. I find
  it extremely hard to believe that you can keep the two separate, and
  going by your posts on your personal blog, you seem to publicly de-
  light in attacking women, the Nebula Awards, our current officers, or
  whatever strikes your fancy. It doesn't fill me with any great hope that
  you can rein in those impulses, and I think your Presidency probably
  would be the worst thing that could ever happen to SFWA.

In light of the uniformly negative response by the members, it will probably not come as a surprise to the reader to learn that I lost the election in a landslide, 444 to 46, to a non-entity who subsequently served a single term that was chiefly notable for his decision to publicly take sides with the publishing giant Hachette against Amazon. Losing the election was not a surprise to me either. In fact, on the very day that I announced my candidacy, I observed the chances of my winning were remote.

> *It is unlikely that I will win the election; even if I win it is unlikely that I can do anything to salvage the situation. The myopic Neo-Luddism and anti-intellectual ideology in the organization appears to be both deep and wide. But I will present my platform to the membership on February 1st so that at least no one will be able to say that things could not have been different if the organization, and the literary genre, continues its downward spiral.*

However, I did expect that after running for office and meeting with overwhelming rejection, such a conclusive result would put an end to the affair and I could go back to being a largely anonymous member of the association. What I didn't realize was that by running for office, I had put a fright into the social justice warriors of SFWA, and they were absolutely determined to put an end to this potential threat to their continued dominance of the organization by any means necessary.

On May 3, 2013, I lost the election. Barely three months later, I received the following email from the successful candidate who had defeated me.

> *The SFWA Board has unanimously voted for your expulsion from the organization, effective immediately. This has been a difficult decision, but thorough examination of the evidence and the situation makes it clear that this action is necessary to best serve the interests of the organization and its members.*

*Sincerely,*
*Steven Gould*
*President*
*Science Fiction and Fantasy Writers of America*

And that's how I came to consciously recognize the First Law of SJW: SJWs always lie. And more importantly, in the process of being subjected to one of their patented swarmings, I learned how to survive and even to thrive in the face of their lies and false accusations.

The goal of this book is to show you how SJWs operate, teach you how to see through their words, explain how to correctly anticipate their actions, and give you the weapons you need to successfully thwart their inevitable attempts to disqualify you, discredit you, and destroy your reputation.

# Chapter 1

# AN INTRODUCTION TO THE SOCIAL JUSTICE WARRIOR

*The new world order of social justice and comradeship, the rational and classless state, is no wild idealistic dream, but a logical extrapolation from the whole course of evolution, having no less authority than that behind it, and therefore of all faiths the most rational.*

—Joseph Needham, *Time: the Refreshing River*, 1943

It begins on a day like any other. You drive to work, listen to the radio as the traffic inches along, park the car when you finally arrive at work, and greet the secretary at the front desk as you walk to your office. You go over your morning emails while drinking from the coffee mug a vendor gave you, and as you're in the middle of writing a reply to one of your accounts, your boss knocks on your open door.

"What's up?" you say without turning around to look at him, continuing to type on your keyboard.

"Do you have some time to stop by my office this morning?" he says.

Something in his voice sounds unusual. You stop typing and turn around. Your eyes narrow. Your boss seems uncomfortable; he doesn't seem to want to meet your eyes.

"Sure, let me just send a few more of these emails that can't wait. Fifteen minutes okay?"

"That will be fine." He's looking strangely cagey. Normally he'll come right in and sit down on the corner of your desk and talk your ear off about the weekend, but now it's as if he can't wait to get out of your office. After ten years at the company, you've got a pretty good sense for when something is taking place behind the scenes among the higher-ups, and now your corporate survival radar is definitely picking up signs of potential trouble on the horizon.

Is it a layoff? Is the company up for sale? Did one of your accounts cancel without telling you? You wrack your brain, but you can't think of any major screwups you might have committed. There was no indication of any disasters looming in your email or on your voice mail this morning. Did Accounting reject your expenses from your last trip to San Francisco? That doesn't seem likely. You didn't even spend your full per-diem!

"So, what's this about, anyway?" You try to make it sound natural, but for some reason, your throat is suddenly dry, and your voice sounds tight.

He looks up and down the hallway before answering. He's hesitant to answer, and when he does, he won't tell you anything. "Well, I'd rather wait until you come to my office to discuss it. I'll see you there in fifteen."

He leaves, and you stare at the empty doorway for a long while, wondering what on Earth that was all about. You turn back to your computer and go through your emails mechanically, your mind still half-occupied with trying to figure out what this mysterious meeting could possibly be about.

Fifteen minutes later, reinforced with a fresh mug of coffee, you make your way to your boss's office with a vague feeling of trepidation.

"Hey, so what's going on?" you say, your voice artificially bright.

"Would you mind closing the door?" your boss says. He's not smiling.

Oh, this is not going to be good, you think, even as you force a smile and comply before taking the empty chair in front of his desk.

He clears his throat. He folds his hands. He forces himself to look at you; he's wearing his serious face, the one you last saw when he announced the most recent round of layoffs. He clears his throat again; it's obvious that he really doesn't want to talk to you about whatever it is. With some difficulty, you resist the urge to tell him to hurry up and get on with it already.

"I'm afraid we've had a complaint about an incident that appears to concern a violation of the company's Code of Conduct last month," he says. "By you."

The Code of Conduct? What the Hell? You're vaguely aware that the company has one; you even read it for laughs one slow afternoon, so you know it's nothing but two pages of meaningless feel-good blather. Equal opportunity, be nice, be respectful, don't discriminate, don't kill anyone, yada yada yada. You're not even sure how anyone in your position could violate the Code of Conduct if he tried, short of stealing something from the company or punching somebody in the face. It's not like you have the power to hire or fire anyone.

And so it begins. Without even realizing it, you have been offered as a sacrifice to that most rational of faiths: social justice.

Six weeks and several meetings with Human Resources later, you're still not entirely sure what happened or exactly what you did to get yourself in trouble. No one will actually tell you anything. You still don't know the name of your accuser (although you've narrowed down the suspects to three likely candidates), and you've been informed that your attendance at an awareness seminar scheduled for this fall will be considered mandatory, but at least you've still got your job. The whispers seem to have stopped and people have largely stopped looking at you funny; it appears you've managed to put the Dead Man Walking stigma behind you.

All in all, everything seems to be back to the way it was before, but with one important exception. You've changed. You're wary now. You walk into work as if entering a minefield. In every conversation, in every meeting, you're careful to watch your every word. Every casual encounter in the hallway becomes a potential confrontation. Every time you meet a co-worker's eyes, you wonder if they are well-disposed or a secret enemy seeking to destroy your job, your career, and your life. You walk on eggshells, and you learn to stop sharing your opinion with anyone about anything, unless it is about something safely innocuous, like sports.

What you don't realize is that you've just survived your first SJW attack. And you're luckier than most. You still have your job, you still have your reputation, and you still have your friends and family. Tens of thousands of people are not so lucky. In the universities, in the churches, in the corporations, in the professional associations, in the editorial offices, in the game studios, and just about everywhere else you can imagine, free speech and free thought are under siege by a group of fanatics as self-righteous as Savonarola, as ruthless as Stalin, as ambitious as Napoleon, and as crazy as Caligula.

They are the Social Justice Warriors, the SJWs, the self-appointed thought police who have been running amok throughout the West since the dawn of the politically correct era in the 1990s. Their defining characteristics:

- a philosophy of activism for activism's sake

- a dedication to rooting out behavior they deem problematic, offensive, or unacceptable in others

- a custom of primarily identifying individuals by their sex, race, and sexual orientation

- a hierarchy of intrinsic morality based on the identity politics of sex, race, and sexual orientation

- a quasi-religious belief in equality, diversity, and the inevitability of progress

- an assumption of bad faith on the part of all non-social justice warriors

- an opinion that motivation matters more than consequences

- a certainty that they are the only true and valid defenders of the op-pressed

- a habit of demanding that their opinions be enshrined as social cus-toms and law

- a tendency to possess a left-wing political identity

- a willingness to deny science, history, logic, their past words, or any other aspect of reality that contradicts their current Narrative.

But there is no need to take my word for it when you can simply read how the SJWs describe themselves, in their own words. This is how one proud, self-declared SJW explained what it means to be a social justice warrior.

> *Being a social justice warrior means taking on a role in this unjust society in which you don't ask for equality but instead, you demand it—and others see that as the "wrong tone." People who think they are doing nothing wrong are going to be upset that we are telling them to change. People are not going to think these problems of inequality are significant because they have the privilege of it not affecting them. They will write us off as radical, overdramatic, and insignificant hypocrites. But social justice warriors must not change their "tone" to appease the oppressor. Oppressors must change, not*

*the oppressed. Being an activist for justice—or a "social justice warrior" if they want to call us that—is about standing up to oppressors… The "wrong" tone is our tone. The wrong tone is the social justice warrior's tone.*

—"On Being A 'Social Justice Warrior'", Austin Bryan,
June 10, 2015

You may not realize that you are an oppressor, but as far as the SJWs are concerned, you are. It doesn't matter if you grew up poor, if you're a minority, if you're handicapped, or even if you can check off most of the victim boxes in the SJW bingo game. If you don't unquestioningly accept the SJW Narrative, then you not only cannot be oppressed, but you have taken the side of the privileged, and in doing so, have become an oppressor yourself.

I am, quite rightly, hated by the SJWs due to my relentless opposition to them. And due to that opposition, the fact that I am an American Indian and that my great-grandfather was a Mexican revolutionary who rode with Pancho Villa means absolutely nothing to them. SJWs seldom hesitate to deny my multiracial heritage and declare that I am a Nazi racist white supremacist bigot who hates Mexicans and every other minority from Arabs to Zulus.

Some of them even go so far as to claim that "race is just a social construct", which explains why an SJW like the NAACP's Rachel Dolezal thought she could get away with blithely telling everyone she was black for years. Unfortunately for her and others like her, genetic science makes it possible to conclusively demonstrate otherwise.

But if SJWs will go so far as to deny the reality of DNA just to disown a badthinking minority, imagine what they're willing to do to those of you who lack the ancestry to play the Red card, the Brown card, or the Black card to neutralize their spurious accusations. (Unfortunately for those of Asian descent, the Yellow card is essentially worthless, as in SJW eyes, Yellow is nothing but an honorary form of White.) The SJW claim to be champions of the underprivileged and oppressed only applies so long as the underprivileged and oppressed dutifully submit to the ideological perspective of their self-declared champions.

Their social justice ideology can be traced back to John Stuart Mill, who conceived a fifth form of justice that was a factual state of affairs versus the four forms of individual conduct that had previously defined the concept. Mill defined this new idea of justice in a form that is still recognizable in the demands of today's SJWs.

> *Society should treat all equally well who have deserved equally well of it, that is, who have deserved equally well absolutely. This is the highest abstract standard of social and distributive justice; towards which all institutions, and the efforts of all virtuous citizens should be made in the utmost degree to converge.*

> —John Stuart Mill, *Utilitarianism*, 1861

As economist F.A. Hayek noted in response nearly 40 years ago, this conception of social justice leads inexorably and invariably towards full-fledged socialism. It is not an accident that the early advocates of social justice were invariably of the political far Left. And while Mill can be excused for his inability to foresee where that highest abstract standard would lead, 26 years after the collapse of the Soviet Union and the intellectual demise of Marxian economics, the SJWs have absolutely no excuse for failing to grasp the undeniable.

But even in Mill's very early formulation, both the totalitarian nature of social justice as well as its orientation towards entryism were apparent. Note that Mill declares that the efforts of the entire virtuous citizenry "should be made" to converge to that goal and that "all institutions" should be directed toward it as well.

Sounds familiar, doesn't it? In a time when every church, every elementary school, every Boy Scout troop, every university, every science journal, every corporation, every movie, every television advertisement, and every video game site are preaching the exact same message of diversity, equality, and tolerance, that century-and-a-half-old declaration sounds ominous indeed.

Submit or be destroyed. That's the real message underlying the superficial one. Conform to their demands or be cast out.

And it is because so many institutions have been made to converge to the social justice cause that sooner or later, no matter what you are or what you do, you will be faced with a choice. Either submit to the SJWs and accept their policing of your every word and thought, or stand against them and endure their attacks.

It's up to you. The choice is yours. As with most such choices, the right choice is not the easy one.

But there is a silver lining. If you make the right choice, if you reject the SJW Narrative and refuse to submit to their demands, you will discover that you are not alone. Not only that, but you will discover that others who have made the same choice have not been destroyed, and have not been cast into outer darkness, but are successfully forging new pathways free of the persistent interference of the SJWs. Men who have been denied platforms have built their own platforms. Women who have removed their children from the SJW propaganda factories are teaching them and raising a new and hardier intellectual elite. Men who have lost their jobs have started their own SJW-free corporations. Women who have lost friends have made new ones and constructed entirely new social circles.

Give a man a platform and he will speak his mind. Deny him a platform, and he will build his own…and you will never silence him again. As one SJW plaintively asked her fellows, "How do you bring the weight of community disapproval on someone who isn't part of the community?"

You don't. Alaric doesn't give a damn that the Romans don't approve.

A broad-spectrum, reality-based resistance to the mirage is now taking shape, a resistance that will eventually undermine and replace all the old institutions that have been invaded and captured by the SJWs. And all it takes to be a part of it is a refusal to accept the religion of social justice, a refusal to bow down before the false gods of Equality, Diversity, Tolerance, Inclusiveness and Progress.

All it takes is the courage to say *non serviam* to the fork-tongued priests of those false gods, the SJWs.

# Chapter 2

# THE THREE LAWS OF SJW

*If you tell a lie big enough and keep repeating it, people will eventually come to believe it. The lie can be maintained only for such time as the State can shield the people from the political, economic and/or military consequences of the lie. It thus becomes vitally important for the State to use all of its powers to repress dissent, for the truth is the mortal enemy of the lie, and thus by extension, the truth is the greatest enemy of the State.*

—Joseph Goebbels, Minister of Public Enlightenment and
Propaganda, *Deutsches Reich*

It is very difficult for a normal person to accept the observable realities of SJW behavior. While everyone lies from time to time, the normal individual very seldom makes statements that can easily confirmed to be false. If you are a normal person, with a normal level of intelligence, you are simply not going to tell anyone that the sky is green and the grass is purple if they can look outside the window and see for themselves that your claim is false. You are not going to tell anyone that your wife is Morgan Fairchild, that Japanese women are taller than Dutch men, or that pregnancy is a social construct instead of a biological reality because you know how easy it would be to prove that what you have said is not true. Even if telling a lie is in your self-interest, it would bother you to be caught lying. It would reduce your credibility in the future, so you avoid telling stupid and obvious lies that are bound to be exposed.

But while normal people avoid telling transparent lies, there are certain groups of people who will make assertions that are observably untrue without hesitation. The insane are one such group, as their grasp of reality is simply unreliable. The sociopathic are another, as their lack of empathy encourages them to tell even the most stupidly obvious lies without any fear of being caught out. The professional propagandists are a third group, as whether they are ad writers, newspaper journalists, or ministers of state, they are paid to construct a new reality, and therefore it is their job to shamelessly disregard the existing one.

The Social Justice Warrior is best regarded as a sort of unpaid amateur propagandist. SJWs are clearly not insane, as their observable discomfort with the more troubling and problematic aspects of reality suffices to demonstrate that they are able to distinguish between that which is real and that which is not. They are also not sociopathic because they are herd animals who are often willing to lie in the perceived interest of the herd-defined narrative, not only in their own immediate interest. Also unlike sociopaths, they are seldom inclined to deny previous statements when caught out but instead tend to respond by moving the goalposts, abruptly falling silent, or otherwise ending the conversation.

It's always fairly obvious on Twitter when an SJW has been caught out, as his first response is usually to block the individual at whom he has been tweeting. Never mind that nine times out of ten, it is the SJW who instigated the conversation.

The reason SJWs are so inclined to make false assertions stems from a motivation that is very similar to that of the professional propagandist, which is the need to disregard existing reality in order to bring about the preferred alternative. In the case of the SJW-preferred reality, this nonexistent alternative is known as the Narrative. The Narrative is the story that the SJWs want to tell. It is the fiction they want you to believe; it is the reality that they want to create through the denial of the problematic reality that happens to exist at the moment. And there is no one definitive Narrative. Instead, there are many Narratives, all of them subject to change at any time, thereby requiring the SJW who subscribes to them to be able to change his own professed beliefs on demand as well.

It may be useful to think of SJWs as a school of hypersensitive fish, every single one of which is capable of rapid changes of direction based on the most minute signals from the fish on either side of them. This is why large numbers of SJWs can go from declaring black to be white to be blue to be red in rapid succession, all without ever appearing to notice that what they are all saying now is completely different than what they were all saying before. And woe to the SJW who fails to keep up and doesn't change his tune in time with the others!

## The First Law

The First Law of SJW is this: *SJWs Always Lie.*

The story that follows is just one example of a journey into the disorienting depths of SJW dishonesty. It's a trivial example of little significance to anyone who was not directly involved, but it is educational and informative in its very triviality because it demonstrates both the absurdities of the Narrative that SJWs attempt to push on everyone as well as the lengths to which they will go to hide the fact that they are lying. Rest assured there is an SJW in your social circle, at your church, or in your office, who is completely capable of behaving in exactly the same way that is described below because the Three Laws of SJW apply to all SJWs. The details are irrelevant, except in that they show the ludicrous extent to which SJWs will go to maintain their sacred Narrative, even when that Narrative is mutating faster than E. coli irradiated at Fukushima Daiichi.

Although I'd been blogging at *Vox Popoli* since October 2003 and had run across more than a few commenters who shamelessly lied and then retreated or fell silent rather than admit that they had done so when their falsehoods were exposed, I didn't begin to realize the full extent to which dishonesty is a fundamental part of the SJW identity until late 2012. That was when on the 25th of December, John Scalzi, a leading SJW in science fiction and a blogger with whom I'd had alternatively civil and uncivil relations over the previous 7 years, happened to brag that his blog, *Whatever*, had just hit 8 million WordPress pageviews for the year. That surprised me, because I'd always assumed that *Whatever* had considerably more readers than 8 million pageviews would suggest. I initially thought that Scalzi must have made a mistake and substituted "pageviews" for "visitors", as my own pair of blogs, *Vox Popoli* and *Alpha Game*, had a combined 5,969,066 Google pageviews in 2011 and were on track to finish with 7,777,620 pageviews in 2012.

It didn't seem possible that I had very nearly the same amount of traffic as the famous blog belonging to the best-selling, award-winning, three-time SFWA President John Scalzi. After all, *Whatever* had been described for years as the biggest blog in science fiction and Scalzi himself was one of Tor Books's top authors, had won a number of literary awards, and was frequently referred to throughout the media as an enormously popular blogger. In fact, just five months before, the *New York Times* had profiled him as a master of buzz and promotion.

> *He is comfortable with the business of promotion: An affable speaker, he is familiar with the patois of fandom and is adept at generating buzz through the nerd mafia of like-minded collaborators. He already reaches up to 50,000 readers a day through his*

*popular blog, "Whatever." ("Taunting the tauntable since 1998"*
*is the slogan on its home page.)*

—"The Extras Get a Life", by John Schwartz,
the *New York Times*, 6 July 2012

Now, I am an economist by training and a game designer by profession. Spotting mathematical anomalies comes quite naturally to me. It's almost automatic. 50,000 readers a day comes to 18,250,000 readers per year, which even the most innumerate individual will notice is considerably more than 8 million. And while that apparent discrepancy could theoretically have been accounted for by the reporter's use of the term "up to", the problem was that as a blogger myself, I knew very well that each reader accounts for multiple pageviews. The average number of daily pageviews per reader for a well-engaged blog, in my decade of experience, is usually somewhere between four and five. So 50,000 readers per day would indicate over 90 million annual pageviews!

So why was John Scalzi bragging about hitting only 8 million pageviews five months later?

Of course, the apparent discrepancy didn't necessarily mean that Scalzi had lied to the reporter. It only meant that he was, at the very least, considerably stretching the truth by referring to one very good day that was at least 9 times better than his average daily traffic. (8 million annual pageviews indicated somewhere between 4,383 and 5,479 readers a day, depending upon exactly how many pageviews per day his readers averaged.) But even a single day with 50,000 readers appeared highly unlikely in light of how the 8 million pageviews represented a sixty percent improvement on his traffic from previous years. Consider the following table of the data that Scalzi provided as part of his 8 million post, to which I have added the number of daily readers that would indicate if each reader accounted for 4.5 pageviews per visit.

*Whatever* site traffic: 2009 to 2012

| Year | Annual Pageviews | Est. Daily Readers |
|------|------------------|--------------------|
| 2012 | *8,000,000* | 4,870 |
| 2011 | 5,409,015 | 3,293 |
| 2010 | 5,131,194 | 3,214 |
| 2009 | 4,488,281 | 2,733 |

Note: *Whatever* actually concluded 2012 with 8,166,822 WordPress pageviews and 4,539 daily readers. It subsequently declined to 7,519,279 pageviews in 2013 and 5,295,655 in 2014.

Having been a blogger for ten years myself, I knew it was very unusual to see even a single day that would double a large blog's average daily traffic, let alone see it jump by a factor of up to 20. Nevertheless, Scalzi continued to not only repeat the claim for the next nine months but even dropped the "up to" qualifier, thereby eliminating any possibility in my mind that he was doing anything but significantly exaggerating his site traffic.

> *John Scalzi @scalzi 6:20 AM—4 Dec 2012*
>
> *Hey, authors of non-traditionally published books! Promote your book to my 50K daily blog readers TODAY*

> *John Scalzi @scalzi 3:33 PM—10 Aug 2013*
>
> *I think if people like the content they will keep coming in regardless. I mean, my site gets 50K readers a day*

My suspicions thereby aroused, I tested the waters by posting several times on this apparent anomaly. This prompted a series of responses that seemed rather bizarre at the time, but which I have since learned are absolutely typical of the SJW who senses that his lies are on the verge of being exposed. In the next section, several of these standard SJW defensive tactics can be observed in addition to a very clear example of the Second Law of SJW in action.

## The Second Law

The Second Law of SJW is this: *SJWs Always Double Down.*

It is important to keep in mind that the SJW concerned had all of the information that I eventually uncovered from the beginning. Nothing that I subsequently learned about John Scalzi and his site traffic was unknown to him, there were no surprises involved, and the only question was whether or not I would be able to unearth the information that would disprove his public claims and expose him as a fraud and a liar. In such a situation, a normal person who has lied—and who knows that his lies have aroused suspicion and are under investigation—is usually inclined to stop lying. In many cases, he will even come clean to the party who is in the process of exposing him and beg for mercy.

Not the SJW. Instead of coming clean in one way or another, the SJW will instead double down and attempt to shore up his lies by concocting an even larger framework of deceit and misdirection to support them. He will throw the full weight of his status and credibility into the effort, call on the support of his entire social network, and try to turn the risk of potential exposure into a popularity contest between him and the individual threatening to expose him. The goal is to destroy the whistleblower's credibility so that even if the truth comes out, no one will believe it.

In this particular case, John Scalzi's first response was to attempt to distract everyone by disqualifying the individual whose uncomfortable questions were threatening the perception of his massive popularity with the public. He did this by pointing to a single controversial comment I had made on my blog in response to a vicious and unprovoked attack by one of his allies, and using it as an excuse to force the SFWA board to choose between me and two of the most influential people in science fiction.

> *My membership is due and I can't in good conscience renew it un-*
> *til SFWA finds the means or moral backbone or whatever's ulti-*
> *mately required to expel someone as hateful and wilfully destruc-*
> *tive as Day—not just from the organisation but from the culture*
> *present within it.*

—John Scalzi, from *Report to the Board of Directors of SFWA*

At the time, John Scalzi was the organization's outgoing three-time president, and Patrick Nielsen Hayden was the Senior Editor and Manager of Science Fiction at Tor Books. Both leading SFWA members, they stopped paying their membership dues that summer and threatened to leave the organization if the Board did not vote to expel me, which it obediently did on August 2013. I was not actually expelled, as Massachusetts state law required a subsequent vote by the entire membership, nor was my expulsion ever publicly announced by the SFWA Board, but apparently the charade of a meaningless vote was sufficient, as both Scalzi and Nielsen Hayden promptly announced they had paid their dues and were once more members in good standing.

*John Scalzi @scalzi 9:18 AM—14 Aug 2013*

*I just renewed my @sfwa membership!*

*P Nielsen Hayden @pnh 11:53 AM—14 Aug 2013*

*@scalzi So did I! What a coincidence! @sfwa*

Having successfully disqualified me in this manner, Scalzi and his allies then proceeded to pretend that my continued attempts to discover the truth about his traffic claims were nothing more than a bitter attempt at revenge for my expulsion from SFWA—never mind that I'd first raised the matter months before the SFWA controversy and I wasn't genuinely expelled from the organization.

His second response was to publicly back off his expanded claims. Four days after I called out the discrepancy between his claimed 50k daily readers and his actual average of around five thousand per day, the "up to" qualifier again began to appear in his statements.

*John Scalzi @scalzi 4:45 PM—16 Aug 2013*

*It's related to having 50K Twitter followers and up to 50K daily readers of the blog, many of whom like SF/F.*

His third response was to attempt to engage in a bit of statistical sleight of hand that did nothing to disprove any of the questions I had raised. Two weeks after the SFWA Board vote, a newspaper published a puff piece on him that led to a number of links from large sites like Daily Kos and produced an incredible spike in his site traffic. He reported that he'd had 60,018 visitors and 100,374 pageviews in a single day, which he promptly screencapped and posted to Twitter.

*John Scalzi @scalzi 12:10 AM—27 Aug 2013*

*All the dudebros who adamantly maintain I don't get 50K visitors a day are totally right. #HAHAHA*

The timing was so perfect in this regard that I actually wondered if he'd somehow managed to plant the story in order to drive his traffic up, but regardless, the fact that he had a single day of 100k-pageview traffic didn't mean that he'd ever previously seen similar traffic. In fact, given the hard limits he'd previously reported, the bigger the spikes were, the lower his average daily traffic would have to be.

Two weeks after that, precisely one month after I'd been "expelled" by the SFWA Board, John Scalzi celebrated having hit 30 million pageviews in six years in an elaborately verbose post designed to further defend his past traffic claims. He even showed a WordPress screenshot to prove that his site had had 30,036,338 pageviews and 349,576 comments over that timeframe.

*At some point yesterday the site passed the 30 million all time views, "all time" in this case defined as "visits recorded by the WordPress stats program since early October 2008," which is when the site switched over to the WordPress VIP hosting service. Note that I would take all stat information with a grain of salt; here is my standard link to explain why. For all that, 30 million views in six years doesn't suck. This 30 million visit milestone happens whilst some folks out there are asserting foamily that I'm lying about my site's visitorship; the bone of contention appears to be that I note the site gets up to 50,000 visitors a day, whilst the foamy folks complain that the daily traffic is in fact nowhere near that, so therefore, I am lying...I don't know about you guys, but I gotta say, if I'm lying about my visitor stats, I'm doing a really terrible job of it. I know. I suck. I must try harder. The good news is, I know of some people who are better at lying about my site stats than I am. Well, maybe "better" isn't the correct term, actually.*

—"30 Million Views", *Whatever,* 13 September 2013

Of course, all this frantic activity, and obfuscation, and misdirection, and name-calling merely served to convince me that the SJW was protesting far too much. Why had he gone to such efforts to get me expelled? Why was he selectively revealing single-day traffic anomalies and long-term traffic totals while steadfastly refusing to simply make his traffic meters public and thereby put a definitive end to the matter? He obviously had the information on hand, so why not click a single button and release it to the public? What purpose could there be to all the dancing if he wasn't trying to hide something?

Sure, 30 million pageviews sounded superficially impressive, as did the 350,000 comments he cited, but then, both numbers had accumulated over a period of six years. I was in a better position to put these numbers in perspective than most because I happened to have over 475,000 comments on my two presumably less-trafficked blogs in only five years. How was it possible for me to have 36 percent more comments in 17 percent less time despite presumably having considerably less site traffic?

The discrepancies were starting to accumulate, and the increasingly wordy, increasingly elaborate defensiveness on Scalzi's part made me increasingly certain that he was lying. But how to prove it to everyone else?

Then it occurred to me that anyone who was willing to shamelessly exaggerate in an interview with the *New York Times* was probably not doing so for the first time. In my experience, most people who are self-promoters never stop promoting themselves. They have a tendency to talk themselves up, and they will often exaggerate when they have no need to do so. Given that the *New York Times* is at the top of the U.S. cultural heap, I figured the chances were very high that Scalzi had similarly inflated his traffic in previous interviews with other reporters. And, sure enough, I found an interview he had given almost exactly three years before to Erin Stocks at a science fiction magazine called *Lightspeed.*

*Anything you ever wanted to know about science fiction writer John Scalzi you can find online at the public and rather opinionated blog that he's kept since 1998,* WHATEVER.SCALZI.COM. *His bio page holds all the usual info—education, past jobs, present jobs, books published, awards won—and is wrapped up with the tongue-in-cheek coda: "For more detailed information, including a complete bibliography, visit the Wikipedia entry on me. It's generally accurate." But spend a little more time browsing, and you'll learn that beyond the dry stats and quippy bon mots, there's more to John Scalzi and his writing than meets the eye. For one thing, his blog gets an extraordinary amount of traffic for a writer's website–Scalzi himself quotes it at over 45,000 unique visitors daily and more than two million page views monthly.*

—"Interview: John Scalzi", *Lightspeed*, September 2010

(Issue 4)

Extraordinary indeed. It's fascinating, isn't it? Three years before the *New York Times* interview that struck me as anomalous, John Scalzi had been publicly claiming to have very nearly the same number of readers, as well as an absolutely impossible number of pageviews. And how could *Whatever* possibly have had "more than two million page views monthly" in September 2010 when he later reported 5,131,194 pageviews for the whole of the year?

At that point I knew, beyond any shadow of a reasonable doubt, that John Scalzi was lying about his site traffic, and what's more, he had been repeatedly lying about it for years. The problem was that in light of that one-day 60k-reader spike, it was still theoretically possible, just barely, that *Whatever* had truly accumulated two million of its five million pageviews in 2010 in a single month. While passing off such an anomaly as an average would be deceptive, it would be technically true. Given Scalzi's known predilection for the absurd "up to" terminology, it wasn't unthinkable. It was the very sort of deceitful word game that he seemed to enjoy playing. And while I very much doubted that explanation was the case here, I couldn't entirely rule it out.

But was it possible to eliminate the possibility? Certainly, if only one could acquire the information contained in *Whatever's* historical site metrics. Every blog owner makes use of various site meters. There are dozens of different meters; the most popular are WordPress and Google Analytics, but there are a considerable number of lesser variants, each of which purports to measure site traffic more accurately than the next. While honest bloggers make their site metrics open to the public, those who wish to maintain some sort of mystique about their traffic and pretend to be more influential than they are tend to lock them down and prevent anyone else from seeing the level of traffic they are actually receiving. Needless to say, John Scalzi made a habit of keeping all of his site meters hidden since it's impossible to exaggerate one's popularity when anyone can see exactly how many visitors and pageviews one's site has.

After 25 years of developing games and designing technologies, I have a fair number of contacts in the technology world. One of them just happened to be an executive at a company whose site meter Scalzi has utilized for years. Since the technology company actually owns the data, it only took a phone call to obtain the historic traffic records for *Whatever* and to compare them with the public numbers he had been reporting. Somewhat to my surprise, the records proved that he had accurately reported the annual numbers for 2009 through 2012, and rather less surprisingly, confirmed he had been lying in his public interviews, on Twitter, and on his blog. They demonstrated very clearly that instead of being as massively popular as everyone, including me, had previously believed, he had been exaggerating his site traffic, by a factor between 7x and 30x depending on whether one looked at pageviews or visitors.

The very month that John Scalzi told *Lightspeed* that *Whatever* had two million pageviews per month, it actually had 305,230. Instead of the "45,000 unique visitors daily" he'd claimed, his site had been averaging 1,808 per day. In June 2012, the last complete month before the *New York Times* interview in which he'd claimed "up to 50,000 visitors per day", his site had 3,260 visitors and 16,356 pageviews per day. (This works out to 5.02 pageviews per visitor, which you may recall is almost exactly at the upper bound of my original estimate.)

I posted the information I'd uncovered on my blog in a chart dating back to January 2009 that showed *Whatever* had only averaged 2,740 readers per day, 47,260 fewer than Scalzi had repeatedly claimed. There was nothing left to debate, obfuscate, misdirect, or deny. The evidence was solid, and the case was closed. John Scalzi had lied, repeatedly, about his site traffic. He wasn't the most popular blogger in science fiction, and his blog did not get "an extraordinary amount of traffic for a writer's website". He wasn't "comfortable with the business of promotion", but was comfortable with lying in order to promote himself.

So, with all the facts out and available for everyone to see, did Scalzi come clean and admit that he'd been repeatedly lying about his traffic in an extraordinarily successful attempt to promote himself as the most popular blogger in science fiction?

Of course not. SJWs never admit their lies even when they're caught red-handed. Which leads us, finally, to the Third Law of SJW.

## The Third Law

The Third Law of SJW is this: *SJWs Always Project.*

Understanding how the Third Law applied in this situation will require a bit of context, so I will briefly provide you with a little background information. For reasons that still remain incomprehensible today, during the leadup to the 2012 American elections, John Scalzi thought it would be clever to post a satirical piece on *Whatever* in which he claimed that he was a rapist. Seriously. I'm not kidding. The piece began in this manner:

> *I'm a rapist. I'm one of those men who likes to force myself on women without their consent or desire and then batter them sexually. The details of how I do this are not particularly important at the moment—although I love when you try to make distinctions about "forcible rape" or "legitimate rape" because that gives me all sorts of wiggle room—but I will tell you one of the details about why I do it: I like to control women and, also and independently, I like to remind them how little control they have.*

—"A Fan Letter to Certain Conservative Politicians", *Whatever*, 25 October 2012

It was a clumsy and remarkably stupid bit of political satire, but I did him the courtesy of taking him at his word and expressed both astonishment and horror at the shocking news that the three-time SFWA President was a self-confessed rapist. I also quoted him, correctly attributed the quote to him, linked to the piece, and dubbed him Rapey McRaperson. McRapey for short. Initially, and for more than a year afterwards, he and other SFWA members attempted to deal with this self-inflicted public relations debacle by pretending that I did not understand satire and acting as if I genuinely believed he was a self-confessed rapist. Now, this is all a bit meta, I know, but bear with me. The story gets downright surreal and there is a dark punchline that no one, least of all me, could have anticipated.

After I successfully exposed Scalzi's fraudulent traffic claims as previously described, he was unable to maintain the pretense of my being satirically challenged any longer and completely changed his tune. He began declaring that I *obviously* understood his confession was mere satire and therefore I was *lying about him*. This was a ridiculous accusation, of course, because I have never met the man and I have absolutely no idea what he has, or has not, done in the past. And while it would certainly be stupid to come out and publicly declare oneself a rapist if one is genuinely a rapist, is it not arguably even stupider to publicly declare oneself to be a rapist if one is not?

Regardless, after so much time had passed, McRapey found it impossible to give up and admit that I had done nothing more than meet satire with satire. After a year of claiming I didn't understand satire, doing so would have made him look foolish and drawn attention to the fact that he had been making light of rape, behavior his fellow SJWs would consider seriously "problematic". So, instead of just admitting that he'd written a prodigiously stupid piece, he concocted a charity drive intended to pressure me to stop calling him "McRapey" and even went on Jian Ghomeshi's popular CBC radio show to complain about how he had been maliciously quoted. The two of them waxed lyrical about how they were both great champions of women's rights and how wonderful it was that the charity proceeds would go to benefit women who had been sexually assaulted. And at one point during the interview, Scalzi was foolish enough to actually say "John Scalzi is a rapist" live on the radio, which is something one should never, ever do if one finds oneself at odds with a member of a techno band.

(If you don't understand why that is something to avoid at all costs, listen to "Everything Has Fallen Into Place" (Groove Kittens mix) by the Pink Rabbit Posse, featuring Rapey McRaperson. It is in astonishingly poor taste and may well be illegal in several European countries, but I guarantee you'll laugh.)

Of course, at no point did John Scalzi ever admit that he'd been caught repeatedly lying about his traffic or that he'd been lying about my inability to understand satire. Instead, he continued trying to revise the Narrative and to portray me as a liar on the radio, in the *Guardian*, on *Whatever*, and on Twitter. Here are a few examples of his revisionist campaign.

- *I assume that for the foreseeable future, Day will continue to lie about me confessing to be a rapist, for his own purposes. Again, annoying. On the other hand, useful. If Day is perfectly happy to lie so baldly and obviously about this particular thing, perhaps that should be considered the baseline for the truth value of any other assertion that he might choose to make, particularly about people.* (27 December 2014)

- *I have an odious bigot spreading obvious lies about me.* (28 December 2014)

- *You appear to have landed on the site of Vox Day. The short version is he's an odious little man who is deeply envious of my career, which he feels he should have, and lies about me a lot to make himself feel better.* (19 February 2015)

The December 27th statement is particularly informative because it shows how the SJW who has been caught lying will immediately resort to a reverse accusation intended to not only cast doubt on the credibility of the accuser, but to call the reliability of the evidence against the SJW into question as well.

While I have repeatedly criticized and made cruel sport of John Scalzi, I have not lied about him. I have no need to do so, and I have backed up every accusation I have ever made against him with either direct quotes or incontrovertible evidence that anyone can independently verify. And yet, instead of admitting that he has lied about me, about himself, and about his site traffic, John Scalzi's only response to being caught repeatedly lying in public has been to stubbornly claim that he is the one being lied about.

This is the Third Law at work. SJWs always project.

This tendency to project their own thoughts, feelings and tendencies on others can be one of the normal individual's most powerful weapons against the SJW. The accusations made by SJWs when they attack others usually reflect, on some level, something they know to be true about themselves. An SJW with creepy tendencies will tend to accuse others of sexual harassment. One who is unsettled in his sexual orientation will often accuse others of homophobia. Female SJWs who feel inferior will accuse men of sexism. And since they are all habitual liars, SJWs find it almost impossible to believe that anyone is ever telling the truth.

In other words, an SJW's accusations will usually tell you where you should start looking in order to expose the SJW's lies.

And as further evidence of the Third Law at work, consider the remarkable punchline to *l'affaire McRapey*. In November 2014, less than two years after John Scalzi appeared on his show to complain about his rape satire being taken at face value, Jian Ghomeshi surrendered himself to the Toronto police. The former CBC radio host is presently awaiting trial on a total of seven counts of sexual assault, and one count of overcoming resistance by choking, against six different women. He faces a maximum possible sentence of life in prison.

The Three Laws of SJW are these:

1. SJWs always lie.

2. SJWs always double down.

3. SJWs always project.

If there is just one thing you take away from this book, it should be that. And if you don't believe me, perhaps you will believe it straight from the SJW's mouth in a statement made before any of the incidents described above took place.

> *I lie, and generally do not regret doing so.*
>
> —John Scalzi, 12 March 2012

.

# Chapter 3

# WHEN SJWs ATTACK

*When people are forced to remain silent when they are being told the most obvious lies, or even worse when they are forced to repeat the lies themselves, they lose once and for all their sense of probity. To assent to obvious lies is to co-operate with evil, and in some small way to become evil oneself. One's standing to resist anything is thus eroded, and even destroyed.*

—Theodore Dalrymple

As you probably know, every day your job and your career are at risk. As teachers, artists, policemen, scientists, and even Nobel Laureates have learned to their dismay, just a single comment made at the wrong time, in front of the wrong individual, is sufficient to destroy a man's reputation and cost him his job. SJWs have refined speech-policing to an extent seldom imagined outside the world of George Orwell's *1984*, and in doing so they have created an *Animal Farm* -like world where some animals are definitely more equal than others.

From the famous and accomplished to the insignificant and the ordinary, absolutely no one is safe. Consider a few of the following examples:

- Dr. James Watson, Nobel Laureate and co-discoverer of DNA, awarded the 1962 Nobel Prize in Physiology or Medicine, forced to resign as chancellor and board member of the Cold Spring Harbor Laboratory after 43 years due to comments he made concerning human biodiversity. The president of the Federation of American Scientists said, "He has failed us in the worst possible way. It is a sad and revolting way to end a remarkable career".

- Brendan Eich, CEO of Mozilla, forced to resign due to a single $1,000 political donation made five years prior.

- Sir Tim Hunt, Nobel Laureate, awarded the 2001 Nobel Prize in Physiology or Medicine, forced to resign from the University College London and fired by the European Research Council's science committee due to a comment about women crying in the laboratory.

- Pax Dickenson, Chief Technology Officer of *Business Insider*, forced to resign due to tweeting several politically incorrect comments.

- Curt Schilling, former Major League Baseball pitcher, baseball analyst, and expert ASL player was suspended by ESPN and removed "from his current Little League assignment pending further consideration" for a single tweet comparing the estimated percentage of Muslims who are extremists to the historical percentage of Germans who were National Socialists.

- North Charleston Police Sgt. Shannon Dildine, fired for wearing Confederate flag boxers.

- Florida high school principal Alberto Iber, fired for defending a Texas police officer accused of racism.

- Greg Elliott, Canadian graphic artist, fired and charged with criminally harassing two female political activists for refusing to endorse their plan to "sic the Internet" on a young man in Northern Ontario who developed a video game of which they disapproved.

Now, many authors might devote a chapter or two to defining what SJWs are, or attempting to explain why they are what they are, or trying to determine why they behave the way they do. I'm not going to do that because it simply isn't relevant to the point of this book. Knowing everything there is to know about shark DNA or what fish grizzly bears prefer to eat doesn't do you any good when you find yourself nose to nose with a hungry one. In like manner, whatever went into making the SJW with whom you are acquainted probably happened decades before you ever met him and there is absolutely no way you are going to undo the consequences of years of psychological aberrancy by reasoning with him or lending him a sympathetic ear.

The SJWs are what they are. They are who they are. It doesn't matter why. All you need to know is that an SJW is an individual who is inclined to thought-police, speech-police, and even race-police everyone around him and will try to marginalize, discredit, and destroy anyone who fails to conform to his thought-policing with sufficient obedience and enthusiasm. All you need to understand about them is enough to be able to recognize one when you see one.

It's not hard. No one but an SJW has ever used more than one of the following words in a sentence: "problematic", "offensive", "inclusive", "triggered" "trigger warning", "privilege", "platforming", "silencing", "equitable", "welcoming", "safe space", "code of conduct", "cisgender", "diversity", "vibrant". No one but an SJW makes quasi-religious fetishes of Equality, Diversity, Tolerance, and Progress.

The most important thing is to grasp the fact that you are never safe in the vicinity of SJWs. Attempting to mollify, appease, or otherwise accommodate the SJWs around you will not put you at any less risk but tends to make you more vulnerable to their attacks in the long run. The phrase "give them an inch, and they will take a mile" might well have been coined to describe SJWs.

This is true even if you are sympathetic to some of the ideas that SJWs claim are their goals, such as equality, diversity, respect, feminism, income equality, fat acceptance, gay "marriage", transgender acceptance, vegetarianism, religious ecumenicism, and atheism. In fact, this is particularly true if you are sympathetic to any of their objectives, as you are more easily pressured and policed.

Normal people assume that SJWs are inclined to take on their ideological opponents, people like me. But the truth is that although they certainly don't like those they invariably label "right-wing extremists", for the most part they leave us alone because we are impervious to their influence. Oh, they will certainly complain about us, take advantage of any tactical missteps on our part, and block us on Twitter, but they very seldom make the sort of concerted effort that one saw in the hounding of Brendan Eich or the metaphorical stoning of Dr. James Watson because they know their efforts will largely be futile.

Instead, they prey on the naïve and the unsuspecting. They prey on the moderates, the middle-grounders, and the fence-sitters. They prey on people like you: good, decent individuals who try to treat everyone fairly and who can't even imagine having done anything that anyone could possibly find objectionable.

Why? Because soft targets are always easier to destroy than hard ones. It's much easier to put pressure on someone who works for a university or a large corporation because the attacking SJW knows that he can count on the support of fellow SJWs in the faculty or the Human Resources department. The bigger the organization, the more likely there is a code of conduct containing nebulous terms that the SJW can claim were violated in some way, shape, or form.

And perhaps most importantly, a target who is psychologically unprepared for being attacked is much more likely to throw up his hands and run away. Look at the list of people above. Aside from the police officer, do any of them strike you as even being right of political center, much less a right-wing extremist? In particular, observe that Watson, Eich, and Hunt all resigned. They were not psychologically ready to deal with the social pressure that is the chief weapon in the SJW arsenal and all three of them rapidly crumbled before it.

Sir Tim Hunt, for example, was so ill-prepared to face the criticism directed at him that he resigned on the basis of a single conversation between an administrative employee and his wife. Contrast that with the hell that I put the SJWs of SFWA through, as the process lasted for months and even forced them to file a DMCA takedown notice with my ISP. I made it so painful for them that by the end, they didn't even dare to put my name in the press release about the board vote. And in the two years since, things have only gone from bad to worse for them.

SJWs always prefer easy targets. And unsuspecting targets are the easiest of them all.

The conventional SJW attack sequence is an eight-step routine that can be observed in most historical SJW attacks. The whole attack sequence is based upon the foundation of a narrative defined by the SJW and is intended to validate that narrative while publicly demonstrating the SJW's power over his target. As you will be able to see, the SJW attack routine is loosely based on Rule 12 of Saul Alinsky's *Rules for Radicals*.

> *Cut off the support network and isolate the target from sympathy.*
> *Go after people and not institutions; people hurt faster than institutions. (This is cruel, but very effective. Direct, personalized criticism and ridicule works.)*

The eight stages of the SJW attack sequence are as follows:

1. Locate or Create a Violation of the Narrative.

2. Point and Shriek.

3. Isolate and Swarm.

4. Reject and Transform.

5. Press for Surrender.

6. Appeal to Amenable Authority.

7. Show Trial.

8. Victory Parade.

## STAGE ONE:
## Locate or Create a Violation of the Narrative

SJWs don't like to be seen as the vicious attack dogs they are because that flies in the face of their determination to present themselves as victims holding the moral high ground. This presents somewhat of a challenge for them, of course, since it is difficult to be proactive about your thought-policing if you need to stand around waiting for someone to victimize you first. SJWs have solved this problem by adopting three standard tactics: self-appointed public defense, virtual victimhood, and creative offense-taking.

They have also invented the useful concept of the "microaggression". This is an inadvertent offense committed by an offender who violates the Narrative without even realizing he has done so. It is the most insidious violation because it means that the hate is buried so deeply inside the offender that he doesn't even realize it is there. Needless to say, SJWs have a highly developed ability to observe these microaggressions being unwittingly committed.

It can be breathtaking to see how an SJW can find an offense being committed by almost anyone doing almost anything. Did you ask someone about his ancestry? That's a racist microaggression because it is offensive to multiracial people to ask them "what" they are. Did you notice someone is black? That's racist. Did you fail to notice someone is black because "you don't see color"? That's racist too. Did you defend yourself against charges of being racist by pointing out that you are married to a black woman? That just shows how racist you truly are because you have objectified a black woman and reduced her to nothing more than a shield to cover your racism. Do you point out that you can't be a white supremacist because you are not white? That's just hiding behind your genes, which is, of course, racist.

We are reliably informed by SJWs that it is a racist microaggression to assume that a person of Hispanic appearance speaks Spanish. It is also racist to assume that a person of Hispanic appearance does not speak English. Your safest bet, one presumes, is to address him in Klingon. Then, when the individual with the bronze complexion suggestive of possible membership in *la raza cósmica* replies with either "what?" or "¿qué?" you will learn how to correctly address him without committing any offensive microaggressions in the process.

In the world of the SJW, being married doesn't mean you don't hate women, having African friends doesn't mean you're not racist, marrying a black woman doesn't mean you're not racist, marrying a Jewish woman doesn't mean you're not anti-semitic, working in an AIDS hospice doesn't mean you're not homophobic, and being black, or Mexican, or Chinese doesn't mean you're not a white supremacist. There is literally no possible defense that anyone accused by an SJW can offer.

In addition to being able to read minds and divine deeply hidden prejudices, SJWs are also walking, talking odioscopes capable of detecting otherwise undetectable hate at microscopic levels of only 15 parts per billion.

This refined ability to detect offense is very important for the SJW because it provides him with a ready excuse to go on the attack against almost anyone while wrapping himself in the virtuous cloak of either a) the noble champion of the downtrodden and oppressed or b) the holy and sanctified victim. While the chosen target may not have violated any social norms perceptible to any sane individual, the SJW's infallible hate-detector will always be able to manufacture something that will justify his launching a campaign of socially just retribution against the offender.

However, SJWs vastly prefer to manufacture mountains out of molehills instead of their own imaginations. They prefer real violations of the Narrative. It's much easier for them to drum up outrage throughout their social circles, and on social media, if the target legitimately gives them something about which to complain. It doesn't have to be much, it doesn't need to be anything significant, but if there is some small action on the part of the target which the SJW can claim, however nonsensically, is in violation of the SJW-declared norms, that makes their case easier.

It can be a political donation of $1,000 to a successful political campaign for which seven million people voted. It can be a joke told at a public speech. It can be a single picture on Facebook. It can be a comment made 26 years ago by your ex-wife. It can even be a tweet that contains nothing but a link. Give them an inch—and the SJWs can whip up a ready-made pogrom in a matter of hours with an impressive degree of shamelessness.

The important thing to note here is that while the violation is always an action, the target is always an individual, and the object is always the casting out of the individual from the organization. The action itself only matters insofar as it indicates that the individual is a Bad Person, and since there is NO PLACE for such Bad Persons in the university, the corporation, the club, the group, or the organization, the only possible solution is for the target to be promptly expelled. And that is why, if necessary, the violation of the SJW

Narrative will be created if it cannot be located.

# STAGE TWO:
# Point and Shriek

Once a violation of the Narrative has been identified, the next step is to summon other SJWs by pointing at the target and shrieking about how terrible, outrageous, and completely unacceptable he is. Again, the actual offense itself doesn't matter and in fact will often be ignored in favor of various accusations of -isms and -phobias and other sins against diversity that clearly indicate what an evil and irredeemable person the target is. Consider the attack on Sir Tim Hunt by Connie St. Louis after the black female lecturer in science journalism at London's City University designated him a target following his address to female journalists at a lunch sponsored by the Women's Science & Technology Associations in Korea. Note that there are no typos in the section below; it precisely replicates the creative approach St. Louis, whose academic qualifications, credentials, and professional resume have been described in the British media as "dubious" and "questionable", takes to the art of punctuation.

> *Nobel scientist Tim Hunt FRS @royalsociety says at Korean women lunch "I'm a chauvinist and keep 'girls' single lab*
>
> *Why are the British so embarrassing abroad? At #WCSJ2015 President lunch today sponsored by powerful role model Korean female scientists and engineers. Utterly ruined by sexist speaker Tim Hunt FRS @royalsociety who stood up on invitation and says he has a reputation as a male chauvinist., He continued "let me tell you about my trouble with girls "3 things happen when they are in the lab; you fall in love with them, they fall in love with you and when you crticize them, they cry" not happy with the big hole he has already*

*dug he continues digging "I'm in favour of single-sex labs"* BUT *he "doesn't want to stand in the way of women. Oh yeah! Sounds like it? let me tell you about my trouble with girls*

*three things happen in the lab: you fall in love with them, they fall in love with you, and when you criticize them, they cry! So as a result, he's in favor of single-sex labs but he doesn't want anything to satnd in the way of women. Really does this Nobel Laureate think we are still in Victorian times???*

—Connie St Louis @connie_stlouis 12:37 AM—8 Jun 2015

She pointed. She shrieked. Her tweet was retweeted 653 times and favorited 211 times. And 31 hours later, her pointing and shrieking was rewarded when the Royal Society took the bait and responded to her on Twitter.

*The Royal Society Verified account @royalsociety 8:26 AM—9 Jun 2015*

*@connie_stlouis @royalsociety is committed to a diverse science workforce. Tim Hunt's comments don't reflect our views*

It was inadvertently brilliant timing on St. Louis's part because Dr. Hunt was flying back to England and did not have a chance to respond publicly to her before it was too late. As Guy Adams described it for the *Daily Mail*, "By the time he touched down at Heathrow, his career and reputation, built up over 50 years, lay in tatters. The days that followed saw him unceremoniously hounded out of honorary positions at University College London (UCL), the Royal Society and the European Research Council (ERC)".

Connie St. Louis's attack on Sir Tim Hunt is the most devastatingly successful example of an SJW point-and-shriek I've ever observed, but all of them more or less follow the same model. The delivery vehicle varies. It may be a tweet, it may be an anonymous note left on an executive's desk, it may be a planted newspaper article, it may be a complaint lodged with the university administration, or it may be a public accusation made before a group of friends. But they all have the same goal in mind, and that is to single out the target and to identify him as someone other SJWs are encouraged to follow the accuser's lead in attacking.

# STAGE THREE:
## Isolate and Swarm

Immediately following on the heels of the Stage Two pointing and shrieking is the third stage. This stage involves two parts, the first of which focuses on the isolation and marginalization of the target, while the second involves overwhelming the target with social pressure brought on by other SJWs and any moderate parties who can be persuaded, or bullied, into joining the witch hunt.

The primary objective of both the isolating and the swarming is to demoralize the target by separating him from anyone who is likely to give him emotional support, and to elicit an apology for his actions. Typically the SJW will have a number of close allies who will immediately leap to the attack on command, and then turn around and cite those allies as evidence that the outrage is widespread and significant in an attempt to turn the "reaction" to the target's offense into a story that will garner media attention. This is particularly effective if the SJW and his allies have connections in various media organizations, which allows them to rapidly transform a minor event into something that is perceived by the public as a major one. The purpose of the media campaign is two-fold: to stamp the Narrative with an "objective" perspective that echoes the SJW's accusations and to let other potential allies know about the hate campaign in the hopes that they will add their weight to the hogpile.

All of the language used to describe the target will be chosen to marginalize him and render him as unsympathetic a figure as possible. These days, it is almost de rigeur to refer to any SJW target as racist, sexist, and homophobic in addition to any specific qualities that may be relevant to the matter at hand; some adventurous SJWs are already adding "transphobic" to the standard list. In fact, this set of accusations is so common now that if you merely type "racist se" into Google, Google will offer to autocomplete the phrase as "racist, sexist, homophobic".

Indeed, the mere act of belonging to a seemingly innocuous group is now sufficient to render one a hateful hate-filled hater; for example, the science fiction SJW Nora Jemisin reliably informs us that not only was Robert Heinlein "racist as *fuck*", but most of science fiction fandom is too. Other groups deemed "institutionally racist, sexist, and homophobic" by SJWs include the Cardiff City football team's management squad, the San Francisco Police Department, the Franciscan Order, the people of Toronto and their mayor, the *Washington Post* editorial page, ad agencies, the Catholic Church, and the Church of Jesus Christ of Latter-day Saints. Among many, many others.

To return to the example of the SJW attack on Sir Tim Hunt, consider the astonishing degree of isolation and swarming that took place as soon as Connie St. Louis pointed and shrieked at him on June 8, 2015. These are just a few of hundreds of similar examples. Note that within 48 hours of the pointing-and-shrieking, the SJWs managed to transform what the *Times* confirmed a month later to be nothing more than a joke that amused the female scientists in the audience into a general indictment on male sexism in science and in society, as well as a revelation of the malicious anti-female hatred long harbored in secret by the dastardly Nobel Laureate. From Twitter to the august pages of the international newspapers, the lynch mob was soon in full cry.

Notice in particular that some of his own SJW colleagues at the Royal Society and University College London were among the first to leap to the attack. Gereint Rees is the Dean of the UCL Faculty of Life Sciences, while David Colquhoun, a fellow of the Royal Society, is also a pharmacologist at UCL.

*The biologist who called female scientists "girls" who fell in love with him then berated them for crying too much isn't an outlier. For females in the science world, sexism is the norm. Lady scientists: they're always falling in love and crying about it. Amiright. So says important man of science, knighted and Nobel Prize-winning biologist Sir Tim Hunt, at a luncheon for science journalists hosted by Korean women scientists.*

—"Nobel Prize-Winning Biologist Calls Women Love-Hungry Crybabies", Brandy Zadrozny, *The Daily Beast*, 9 June 2015

*The British scientist, who won the 2001 Nobel Prize in medicine, was giving a talk at a journalism conference when he expressed his support for sex-segregated labs and admitted he has a reputation as a misogynist. A Nobel laureate has come under fire for shockingly sexist remarks at the World Conference of Science Journalists in Seoul, South Korea.*

—"Nobel Prize Winner Makes Shockingly Sexist Remarks At Journalism Meeting", Cat Ferguson, *BuzzFeedNews*, 9 June 2015

*Ana Gomez (@anacrgomez) 9 June 2015*

*Here is Tim Hunt, a Nobel winning biologist, trying to make his nose hair not be the most disgusting thing about him*

*Mats Grahn (@Mats Grahn) 9 June 2015*

*Revoke the Nobel prize awarded to Tim Hunt. His contribution to science cannot outweigh the damage he has done*

*David Colquhoun (@david_colquhoun) 9 June 2015*
*The Royal Society is quick of the mark in dissociatiing itself from Tim Hunt's dreadful comments #HUNTGATE*

*Geraint Rees (@profgeraintrees) 9 June 2015*
*@ucl Faculty of Life Sciences totally rejects the comments allegedly made by Sir Tim Hunt FRS today. Science needs women @royal-society*

*David Colquhoun (@david_colquhoun) 9 June 2015*
*David Colquhoun retweeted Geraint Rees. Very glad to see my dean coming out swinging on the Hunt affair*

*Dorothy Bishop (@deevybee) 9 June 2015*
*@profgeraintrees Could we ask that he not be on any appointments or promotions committees, given his views*

*This is a moment to savour. Hunt has at last made explicit the prejudice that undermines the prospects of everyone born with child-bearing capabilities. It is not men who are the problem, it is women! So here's a hypothesis, Sir Tim. It's not the women who are the problem. It's you.*

    —"Tim Hunt, where's the science in your prejudice against women?", Anne Perkins, the *Guardian*, 10 June 2015

*David Colquhoun, emeritus professor of pharmacology at University College London, said Hunt's comments were a "disaster for the advancement of women". Hunt's words have also been roundly criticised by female scientists on Twitter. One woman, a postdoctoral researcher, tweeted: "For every Tim Hunt remark, there's an extra woman in science that takes an interest in feminism. Ever wonder why there are so many of us?" Hunt, who won the Nobel Prize for discovering protein molecules that control the division of cells, could not be contacted for a comment.*

—"Nobel scientist Tim Hunt: female scientists cause trouble for men in labs", Rebecca Radcliffe, the *Guardian*, 10 June 2015

*Tim Hunt complained that female scientists "cry" and make male colleagues fall in love with them... The Royal Society, of which Hunt is a fellow, quickly tweeted a message distancing itself from Hunt's remarks, writing that the comments "don't reflect our views" and later adding, "Science needs women."*

—"A Nobel Scientist Just Made a Breathtakingly Sexist Speech at International Conference", Alissa Greenberg, *TIME*, 10 June 2015

*Aaron Mifflin (@aaron_mifflin) 10 June 2015*

*Not surprisingly, most women I know also have a rule that states they shouldn't have #TimHunt in their labs.*

# STAGE FOUR:
## Reject and Transform

Sir Tim Hunt apologized for his remarks almost immediately. So did James Watson. So did Brendan Eich. But SJWs don't seek apologies for the same reason normal people do. They don't demand apologies in order to see that the individual who has offended them admits that he has commited an offense, regrets having done so, and will seek to avoid doing so again in the future.

The reason SJWs demand apologies is in order to establish that the act they have deemed an offense is publicly recognized as an offense by the offender. The demand for an apology has nothing whatsoever to do with the offender. It is focused on the SJW's need to prove that the violation of the Narrative involved is publicly accepted as a real and legitimate offense for which punishment is merited. And once the apology is duly delivered by the accused, who is usually bewildered at the accusation and in a state of shock at the unexpected social pressure he faces, it is promptly rejected because it is not the action, but the actor, that is the real target.

Keep in mind that it is not in the interests of the SJWs to accept the apology anyhow, because if the action that violated the Narrative can be forgiven, that will limit its utility to use against others who reject the Narrative in the future. What use is it to go through the whole process of publicly crucifying a Nobel Prize winner if you're only going to let him off the cross when he says he is sorry? After all, Voltaire didn't observe that the Royal Navy found it necessary to *criticize* an admiral from time to time to encourage the others, he observed that the British found it necessary to *kill* one.

The ultimate purpose of an SJW attack is not to destroy the individual attacked, but rather to make an example of him that will dissuade others from violating the SJW Narrative in a similar fashion. And that is why it is absolutely and utterly futile for the target of an SJW attack to apologize for whatever offense he is said to have caused.

Consider the sequence of events in three of the most significant SJW lynchings in recent years. In each case, the sequence is the same.

1. SJWs attack a statement or action by the target.

2. The target apologizes in the hope of resolving the situation.

3. The apology is deemed to be insufficient or irrelevant in some way, and the social pressure actually increases.

4. The target is destroyed.

James Watson, Brendan Eich, and Tim Hunt all apologized. And as the following pairs of quotes should suffice to demonstrate, they really need not have bothered doing so.

## James Watson: apology and result.

*James D. Watson, who shared the 1962 Nobel prize for deciphering the double-helix of DNA, apologized "unreservedly" yesterday for comments reported this week suggesting that black people, over all, are not as intelligent as whites... Late yesterday, the board of Cold Spring Harbor Laboratory, a research institution in New York, issued a statement saying it was suspending the administrative responsibilities of Dr. Watson as chancellor "pending further deliberation."*

—"Nobel Winner Issues Apology for Comments About Blacks", Cordelia Dean, the *New York Times*, 19 October 2007

*James Watson, the world-famous biologist who was shunned by the scientific community after linking intelligence to race, said he is selling his Nobel Prize because he is short of money after being made a pariah. Mr Watson said his income had plummeted following his controversial remarks in 2007, which forced him to retire from the Cold Spring Harbor Laboratory on Long Island, New York... "Because I was an 'unperson' I was fired from the boards of com-*

*panies, so I have no income, apart from my academic income," he said.*

—"James Watson selling Nobel prize", Keith Perry, *The Telegraph*, 28 November 2014

## Brendan Eich: apology and result.

*I am deeply honored and humbled by the CEO role. I'm also grateful for the messages of support. At the same time, I know there are concerns about my commitment to fostering equality and welcome for LGBT individuals at Mozilla. I hope to lay those concerns to rest, first by making a set of commitments to you. More important, I want to lay them to rest by actions and results. A number of Mozillians, including LGBT individuals and allies, have stepped forward to offer guidance and assistance in this. I cannot thank you enough, and I ask for your ongoing help to make Mozilla a place of equality and welcome for all. Here are my commitments, and here's what you can expect:*

*Active commitment to equality in everything we do, from employment to events to community-building.*

*Working with LGBT communities and allies, to listen and learn what does and doesn't make Mozilla supportive and welcoming.*

*My ongoing commitment to our Community Participation Guidelines, our inclusive health benefits, our anti-discrimination policies, and the spirit that underlies all of these.*

*My personal commitment to work on new initiatives to reach out to those who feel excluded or who have been marginalized in ways that makes their contributing to Mozilla and to open source difficult.*

*I know some will be skeptical about this, and that words alone will not change anything. I can only ask for your support to have the time to "show, not tell"; and in the meantime express my sorrow at having caused pain.*

—"Inclusiveness at Mozilla", Brendan Eich, BRENDANEICH.COM, 26 March 2014

*Russell Beattie (@RussB), 27 March 2014*

*Call me crazy, but I was looking for an unconditional apology from Eich, as well as a substantial monetary donation as a show of contrition.*

*Eich was apparently pushed out by the board… Though Eich apologized for causing "pain" and insisted he could separate his personal views from the way he ran the company, that didn't wash with the board.*

—"Mozilla's Brendan Eich: Persecutor Or Persecuted?", Susan Adams, *Forbes*, 4 April 2014

## Sir Tim Hunt: apology and result.

*The Nobel laureate Tim Hunt has apologised for comments he made about female scientists. Speaking on BBC Radio 4's Today programme on Wednesday, Hunt apologised for any offence, saying he meant the remarks to be humorous—but added he "did mean the part about having trouble with girls".*

*The Royal Society distanced itself from Hunt's comments. It said: "The Royal Society believes that in order to achieve everything that it can, science needs to make the best use of the research capabilities of the entire population. "Too many talented individuals do not fulfil their scientific potential because of issues such as gender and the society is committed to helping to put this right. Sir Tim Hunt was speaking as an individual and his reported comments in no way reflect the views of the Royal Society."*

—"Tim Hunt apologises for comments on his 'trouble' with female scientists", Jamie Grierson, the *Guardian*, 10 June 2015

*After intense criticism for undeniably sexist comments he made about female scientists, Nobel Laureate Tim Hunt offered up an apology that really only made him look worse.*

—"Nobel Laureate Tim Hunt Under Fire For Sexist Comments", Abigail Tracy, *Forbes*, 10 June 10, 2015

*In a statement published on its website UCL said that it could confirm that Hunt had resigned on Wednesday from his position as honorary professor with the UCL Faculty of Life Sciences, "following comments he made about women in science at the World Conference of Science Journalists on 9 June". It added: "UCL was the first university in England to admit women students on equal terms to men, and the university believes that this outcome is compatible with our commitment to gender equality."*

—"Nobel laureate Tim Hunt resigns after 'trouble with girls' comments", Ben Quinn, the *Guardian*, 11 June 2015

Watson's apology could not have been more abject. Eich's sincerity and abasement before the thought police could not have been more genuine or more groveling. Hunt's apology could not have come more quickly. Yet none of them proved sufficient to even marginally reduce the amount of social pressure the SJWs continued to bring to bear on them—pressure that none of them proved able to successfully withstand.

# STAGE FIVE:
## Press for Surrender

Once the apology has been duly offered, and rejected, ignored, or transformed into a prosecutorial brief, the SJWs promptly begin to close for the kill. In most cases, the true-believing SJWs are not in a position to directly enforce their will. While those who are in positions of executive authority at corporations, universities, and other influential organizations are usually sympathetic to the SJW Narrative, and duly recite the organization's commitment to diversity, equality, tolerance, vibrancy, feminism, and whatever other dogmas the SJWs have managed to slip into the organization's code of conduct, they are seldom outright SJWs, and they are often caught nearly as off-guard by the manufactured outrage as the target himself.

This is more true in the corporate world and in the church than in academia or government agencies, where decades of affirmative action, institutional leftward bias, and the lack of objective performance metrics have rendered the decision-makers hypersensitive to the demands of their most problematic underlings. That's why a schoolteacher or even a school principal is much more likely to be fired for a much less egregious violation of the Narrative than a corporate employee or a pastor. In fact, in many state and local governments, you are far more likely to be fired for violating the Narrative than you are for never coming in to work at all, especially if you are a member of one of the Narrative-protected classes. Crying "discrimination" to a mid-level manager at a state government agency is more effective than throwing garlic-infused holy water in the face of a vampire.

But in most organizations, firing someone involves a fair amount of tedious paperwork, as well as an amount of evidence documenting unprofessional behavior in the workplace. Since in most places "violating the Narrative" is only a firing offense in SJW minds, and since some perception of people being free to do and say what they want in their off-hours still persists, the SJWs know that for all their massed outrage and social pressure, actually getting someone fired is usually a difficult, lengthy, and uncertain process.

That is the primary reason they always push very hard for the individual to voluntarily resign. There is a secondary reason too; if the target resigns, the SJWs can wash their hands of any responsibility for the resignation and pretend that the whole affair was merely a private, personal decision on the part of the successfully executed target—a decision that had nothing whatsoever to do with the social pressure to which he'd just been subjected. SJWs are like a firing squad that offers its blindfolded victim a loaded pistol and then, after a single gunshot rings out, walks away pretending that the victim committed suicide for reasons that no one could possibly know.

SJWs always lie. Consider the crocodile tears of the SJW who led the initial charge against Brendan Eich, tears he shed only after the Mozilla board pressured the CEO into resigning.

> *I want to say how absolutely sad to hear that Brendan Eich stepped down. I guess this counts as some kind of "victory," but it doesn't feel like it. We never expected this to get as big as it has and we never expected that Brendan wouldn't make a simple statement. I met with Brendan and asked him to just apologize for the discrimination under the law that we faced. He can still keep his personal beliefs, but I wanted him to recognize that we faced real issues with immigration and say that he never intended to cause people problems. It's heartbreaking to us that he was unwilling to say even that.*

—"A Sad 'Victory'", Hampton Catlin, *Rarebit*, 3 April 2014

Mark Surman, the Executive Director of the Mozilla Foundation, which appoints and is responsible for the Mozilla Board that forced Eich to resign, similarly attempted to wash his hands of the matter. No doubt he was influenced in this regard by the 47,491 messages, most of them highly negative, that inundated Mozilla in response to Eich's resignation.

> *As I look at the world's reaction to all this, I want to clarify... Brendan Eich was not fired. He struggled to connect and empathize with people who both respect him and felt hurt. He also got beat up. We all tried to protect him and help him get around these challenges until the very last hours. But, ultimately, I think Brendan found it impossible to lead under these circumstances. It was his choice to step down.*

Notice how the focus is placed on the "choice" to step down, never mind the intense social pressure being placed on him by the very SJWs who profess to be sad after they achieve their objective and acquire the scalp they are seeking.

And Surman was right to be concerned about the public's reaction to the Mozilla CEO's forced resignation, which is why he tried to dissemble. Mozilla Firefox's user base was already in decline before SJW attack on Eich, and it declined even more precipitously in the months that followed. While Connie St. Louis's reaction to being asked about taking down a Nobel Laureate was different, note that she similarly attempted to decline any responsibility for the knife sticking out of her victim's back.

> *Asked yesterday if she regretted Sir Tim losing his job, the lecturer in science journalism replied: 'I've no regrets about breaking a journalistic story. This is about journalism. Secondly it's about women in science. My intention was not for him to lose anything. But he didn't lose anything. He resigned.'*

> —"Lecturer who revealed Sir Tim Hunt's 'sexist' comments says she has no regrets about costing the Nobel Prize winner his job", Colin Fernandez, the *Daily Mail*, 25 June 2015

Perhaps "wiping the fingerprints off the murder weapon" would be a better way to describe the final aspect of the fifth stage of an SJW attack, but regardless, the lesson is clear. Forcing a resignation is an SJW's primary objective and ideal victory condition, whether he sees fit to feign regret and sorrow in the aftermath or not.

# STAGE SIX:
## Appeal to Amenable Authority

Of course, not everyone is taken completely off-guard by an SJW attack. In my case, I'd been repeatedly attacked by the SJWs in SFWA for a period of 8 years before I slipped up and gave them just enough ammunition to take the intensity of their attacks to a new level. In like manner, and despite being one of the magazine's more popular and intelligent contributors for over a decade, John Derbyshire had long been viewed as something of a loose cannon by the editors at *National Review* for his failure to abide consistently by the SJW Narrative there. While *National Review* is a nominally conservative magazine and often criticizes political correctness, its editors are generally far to the left of its readers and its contributors alike, and they have been known to engage in an amount of thought-policing, especially when it comes to racial matters or the subject of Israel.

On April 4, 2012, Derbyshire published a piece on Taki's Magazine called "The Talk: Nonblack Version". It was little more than an advice piece for white and Asian parents to give to their children mirroring the hypothetical talk some black columnists claimed black parents were giving their children to warn them about the potentially lethal racism of whites following the much-publicized death of Trayvon Martin.

As you'd expect, the SJWs promptly attacked, with calm and thoughtful articles such as "Racist John Derbyshire Writes Most Racist Article Possible, Pegged to Trayvon Martin Case" on *Gawker*, "National Review writer ignites firestorm over 'disgusting rant' on race" in the *Guardian*, "How to succeed in racism without really trying: John Derbyshire tells his children to stay away from black people" in *The New York Daily News*, "John Derbyshire's Advice on How to Talk to Your Children About Black People" in *The Observer*, "National Review Writer Tops Racism With More Racism" on *ThinkProgress* and "National Review's John Derbyshire Pens Racist Screed: 'Avoid Concentrations Of Blacks,' 'Stay Out Of' Their Neighborhoods" on *The Huffington Post*.

What was interesting about literally all of these articles was the particular stress that they placed on the fact that John Derbyshire was a writer for *National Review*. Some of them, including a few that directly referred to *National Review* in the title, did not even mention the fact that the article that so egregiously violated the Narrative was written for *Taki's Magazine*, not *National Review*.

The reason for this otherwise inexplicable anomaly is easily understood once you grasp that the purpose of an SJW attack is to destroy the career of the target. John Derbyshire is an experienced, tough-minded veteran commentator who has survived many a critical attack. Taki, the publisher of the magazine named after him, is a wealthy iconoclast who is neither susceptible to social media pressure nor subject to the need to appease corporate advertisers. The SJWs attacking Derbyshire knew perfectly well that the man who once played a thug in Bruce Lee's *Return of the Dragon* wasn't about to burst into tears and resign simply because he faced a hailstorm of SJW outrage. They also knew that Taki was considerably more likely to laugh at them, give Derbyshire a raise, sprout angel's wings, and then ascend to the peak of Mount Olympus, than to give into their demands to fire him.

But *National Review* was a considerably softer target. It was already somewhat notorious on the political right for its periodic purges, having previously purged Joe Sobran, its former editor, in 1993, another former editor, Peter Brimelow, in 1997, and Ann Coulter, the popular conservative columnist, in 2001. It was no accident that the SJWs attacking Derbyshire went out of their way to use the *Taki* article to link *National Review* and racism together; they know that media conservatives have historically been frightened to death about being labeled as racist and are willing to do nearly anything to avoid being accused of the dread r-word. And, indeed, various *National Review* editors and writers nearly tripped over each other in their rush to be the first to denounce Derbyshire.

Editor Rich Lowry criticized Derbyshire's "appalling view of what parents supposedly should tell their kids about blacks" while Ramesh Ponnuru publicly distanced himself from Derbyshire on Twitter. Jonah Goldberg, who, ironically enough, is well-known for his national bestseller entitled *Liberal Fascism*, declared, "I find my colleague John Derbyshire's piece fundamentally indefensible and offensive. I wish he hadn't written it."

Unsurprisingly, it didn't take long for the SJWs to crack *National Review*. Only four days after the piece was published, Rich Lowry released a prim and cowardly statement purging *NR*'s long-time contributor in a mendacious manner worthy of an SJW.

> *Anyone who has read Derb in our pages knows he's a deeply literate, funny, and incisive writer. I direct anyone who doubts his talents to his delightful first novel, 'Seeing Calvin Coolidge in a Dream,' or any one of his 'Straggler' columns in the books section of NR. Derb is also maddening, outrageous, cranky, and provocative. His latest provocation, in a webzine, lurches from the politically incorrect to the nasty and indefensible. We never would have published it, but the main reason that people noticed it is that it is by a National Review writer. Derb is effectively using our name to get more oxygen for views with which we'd never associate ourselves otherwise. So there has to be a parting of the ways. Derb has long danced around the line on these issues, but this column is so outlandish it constitutes a kind of letter of resignation. It's a free country, and Derb can write*

*whatever he wants, wherever he wants. Just not in the pages of NR or NRO, or as someone associated with NR any longer.*

Thus emboldened, SJWs were inspired to increase the pressure and managed to claim the scalp of a second NR contributor, University of Illinois professor emeritus Robert Weissberg, just three days later. They even took a crack at long-time *National Review* editor-at-large John O'Sullivan, CBE and former special adviser to Prime Minister Margaret Thatcher, but sanity prevailed. The purges were not ended, however, as Managing Editor Jason Lee Steorts fired *NR*'s most popular writer, Mark Steyn, two years later, in 2014.

Frankly, it's a wonder anyone still reads *National Review*, as the talent they've purged over the years is considerably more impressive than the sum total of the talent they've retained. Jonah Goldberg and Kevin Williamson aside, few must-reads remain. The important thing to learn from the Derbyshire purging, however, is that SJWs will always appeal to the most amenable authority rather than the most relevant or the most obvious. They will always aim for the weakest support and focus their malicious efforts there.

# STAGE SEVEN:
# Show Trial

In Stalin's Soviet Union, it was common for the People's Commissariat for Internal Affairs, or NKVD, to arrest people, put them on public trial for crimes that were mostly fictional, and then execute them. In just two years, 1.5 million people were arrested, and 681,692 of them were executed. The NKVD could be remarkably creative in this regard; in one famous case, they invented a political party with a name taken from a science fiction novel written by Alexander V. Chayanov, the "Labour Peasant Party", and then put

Chayanov and others on trial for belonging to the criminal yet non-existent party!

This stage of the SJW attack sequence can take several different forms. But what they all have in common is that the outcome is always predictable and the target is always found guilty. Even when the accuser is of deeply dubious credibility, the accusation will be taken as seriously as a *Rolling Stone* reporter listening to a college girl claiming to have been raped by fraternity brothers.

For example, the *Daily Mail* conclusively documented that Sir Tim Hunt's accuser, Connie St. Louis, had misrepresented herself on her resume on London's City University website, never written the book that she was given £50,000 to write by the Joseph Rowntree Journalist Fellowship, required 30 ex post facto editorial revisions to her *Guardian* piece about the Hunt affair, and had her account of Hunt's behavior at the Korean luncheon directly contradicted by a number of female journalists at the event as well as a recording that surfaced more than a month after Hunt had already resigned or been fired from his various posts.

St. Louis was an unreliable witness for the prosecution, to put it mildly. Nevertheless, despite support for Hunt's reinstatement from the Lord Mayor of London and well-known scientists such as Bryan Cox and Richard Dawkins as well as broadcaster Jonathan Dimbleby, Michael Arthur, the UCL President & Provost, refused to consider it, declaring that "reversing that decision would send entirely the wrong signal" and that UCL's "commitment to gender equality and our support for women in science was and is the ultimate concern". Apparently, as far as UCL is concerned, science needs women more than it does Nobel Prize winners. Just to add insult to injury, the 20-member UCL Council met a few weeks later to reaffirm and unanimously support the university's acceptance of Hunt's resignation.

After all, it was his decision to resign, right? The fact that he was coerced into resigning by a threatening call made to his wife, who was told that Hunt would be fired if he didn't resign, was completely swept under the carpet and ignored by the Provost and the Council alike. This was not surprising. The verdict of the SJW show trial is always predetermined, and any appeals, however well-documented, are certain to fail.

## STAGE EIGHT:
## Victory Parade, or, The Ritual Display of the Corpse

In medieval times, it was common for the bodies of executed criminals to be displayed in public in order to deter anyone who might be tempted to commit similar crimes. This was known as "gibbeting" and refers to the mechanism from which the corpses of the criminals were hung when put on display. SJWs don't physically gibbet their victims, but they certainly do so metaphorically, as once the surrender (i.e. resignation) has been achieved or the show trial has been completed and the execution (i.e. firing) has taken place, they repeatedly display the corpse in a ritual manner, to demoralize anyone else who might otherwise be inclined to challenge their Narrative.

Wikipedia is their favored gibbet. If you visit the Wikipedia page devoted to anyone who has been successfully attacked by SJWs, you will find that a significant portion of their page is dominated by the so-called news of their downfall. It doesn't matter if they are otherwise notable for discovering DNA, winning Nobel Prizes, or writing science fiction novels, the SJWs utilize Wikipedia as a primary means of ensuring that every time anyone looks up information about the individual, one of the first things they will see is the fact that the SJWs successfully attacked them.

More than two thousand words, nearly 20 percent, of the Wikipedia page about James Watson are devoted to "Controversies", and the reference to his resignation is supported by no less than 17 separate citations from reliable sources, which is 14 more than anything related to his discovery of the DNA molecule's structure or any of his other scientific or personal

achievements. As an aside, it's worth mentioning that the oversourcing of
critical citations is a reliable indicator that an individual on Wikipedia is
hated by the SJW admins there; on the page about me, four separate sources
were cited in order to establish the very important historical fact that after
being nominated for a minor literary award in 2014, I finished last, behind
No Award, a feat I managed to achieve again in 2015.

As of this writing, 55 percent of the Wikipedia page about Sir Tim Hunt,
PhD, cancer researcher, Royal Fellow, Knight Bachelor, husband, father, and
Nobel Prize-winner, concern "Remarks about women in science". Of the
517 total edits to that page since it was first created in 2005, 318 were made
in the first five weeks after his comments at the Korean luncheon.

These Wikipedia gibbets are then used to seed articles in various media
all around the world. When I was interviewed in Paris by *Le Monde* after
hosting a #GAMERGATE event there, literally the first thing the French reporter covering the event asked me about was the "Conflict with the SFWA"
section from the Wikipedia page about me, despite the fact that the events it
related had taken place years before and had absolutely nothing to do with
#GAMERGATE, my 25-year career in the game industry, or the event.

In the case of more noteworthy victims, the Victory Parade is also used to
launch more general attacks and to justify political action supported by the
SJWs in the media. For example, several days after Sir Tim Hunt resigned
from UCL and was no longer a legitimate news story in himself, his remarks
were still being pilloried by SJWs in the British media, who found them
to be a useful tool for attacking city workers, senior members of the UK
Independence Party, the Metropolitan police, scaffolders, the judiciary, the
military, Sky Sport, the technology industry, all sporting organisations, and
the BBC, as well as an excuse to call for a female leader of the Labour Party.

*All the time, for instance, that BBC producers wondered, aloud,*
*if a woman could ever be tough enough to conduct a competent*
*interview, Hunt, the Nobel prize winner, was in his laboratory,*

*quietly wishing the "girls" would pack up their Bic for Her along with their smelling salts, and, to use the biochemical jargon, bugger off... As disheartening as it is, that Labour's choice of replacements should be composed of uniformly uninspiring politicians, talking mainly indistinguishable gibberish, the party finally has a chance to pick a woman leader, and given current levels of unapologetic sexism, it is hard to see any reason not to.*

—"Sexist remarks are just the tip of an ingrained culture",
Catherine Bennett, the *Guardian*, 13 June 2015

But although this 8-stage attack sequence applies to most SJW attacks, the real problem with them doesn't have anything to do with those of us who are sufficiently well known to draw hostile media attention. The real problem is how many people suffer the malicious attention of the thought police without anyone knowing about it at all. We don't know how many Americans lose their jobs every year due to SJW attacks, but we do know that there are an average of 25,000 criminal charges being laid every year in Britain for speech offences and that over 12,000 of those judicial proceedings result in convictions.

The SJWs are "an army of self-appointed militants who see themselves as the guardians of correct thinking", and their culture of thuggish speech-policing is on the verge of taking over society, if it has not already. Fortunately for both free speech and society, after 20 years of rampaging freely from one victory to the next, the SJWs have finally met with an implacable and ruthless enemy against whom their social pressure is impotent and their media dominance has proven meaningless.

# Chapter 4

# COUNTERATTACK

*I don't agree with what you say and I will defend to the death the abuse and vitriol you receive for saying it.*

—Godfrey Elfwick

In 2012, a fat and unattractive woman with blue hair and numerous piercings decided to play at being a "game designer". She plugged forty thousand words into the Twine engine, a hypertext tool that allows people without any knowledge of programming to create interactive fiction games similar to Zork and other text adventures circa 1977, combined it with a ten-second piano loop, and called it a game.

The "game", *Depression Quest*, is described as "an interactive fiction game where you play as someone living with depression. You are given a series of everyday life events and have to attempt to manage your illness, relationships, job, and possible treatment."

It's even less fun than it sounds and is little more than a digital *Choose Your Own Adventure* book that tracks just three variables: how depressed you are, if you are seeing a therapist, and if you are on medication. Accompanied by a droning piano repeating the same notes over and over and over again, it repeatedly tells you how horribly unhappy you are while giving you the opportunity to make choices such as deciding whether or not to tell your mother that everything is fine. I have never played a less entertaining computer game, which is saying something considering that I was once forced to review *Inferno*, ranked as the 44th worst game of all time, for *Computer Gaming World*. Below is a typical status report from *Depression Quest*, which should by rights have been called *Alpine Adventure: The Quest for Dignitas*.

> *You are very depressed. You spend a large amount of time sleeping, hating yourself, and have very little motivation.*

Remarkably, astoundingly, *unbelievably,* the "game", to the extent one could even call it that, not only garnered several independent game awards but also received unexpectedly favorable media attention despite overwhelmingly negative reactions from the gamers who actually played it. On *Metacritic*, which aggregates critical and player reviews, its user score is 1.8 out of 10 and is summarized as "Overwhelming dislike based on 308 Ratings." Nevertheless, despite being soul-drainingly boring and more than three decades technologically out-of-date, *Depression Quest* was somehow deemed to be genuine game news and was repeatedly mentioned by *Polygon*, *Rock Paper Shotgun*, and *Kotaku*, as well as a number of other game sites.

Other than mystifying every single gamer who happened to read about it, no one played *Depression Quest* or paid its developer any significant attention until August 2014, when an upset young man who had finally broken it off with his cheating girlfriend created a WordPress blog called *The Zoe Post* that documented, in excruciating detail, his experience of having loved and lost.

> *Sometime around November of 2013, I signed up for an OKCupid account and got a 98% match with a cutie with colorful hair (cool), who was super into social justice stuff (good!), and was super into video games (neat!), and liked to make them (ah! I used to make them, that was fun times!), and by some coincidence turns out to*

*have made a somewhat esoteric game I happened to have played a while back.*

That "somewhat esoteric game" was *Depression Quest*. What caught the industry's attention was that the flagrant cheating of which Eron Gjoni complained involved five different men, at least three of whom were involved in the game industry. One of those men subsequently hired the girlfriend in question, and, more significantly, another one was a game journalist who had written for *Rock Paper Shotgun* prior to moving to *Kotaku*. Given the very poor quality of *Depression Quest*, it seemed readily apparent to casual observers that the unusual amount of media attention garnered by the game must have been the result of the developer's liberal distribution of her sexual favors. While this does not appear to have exactly been the case (and I have never bothered to sort out exactly who was having sex with whom, and when), there was no doubt that a number of ethical lines had not so much been crossed as completely obliterated.

And that's when everything started to get truly weird.

Game journalists reacted to the gaming public's attacks on the game media by lining up solidly behind Depression Quest and its neophyte female developer. Unexpectedly, so did 4chan, a popular site with a sizable gaming contingency that had previously been ground zero for anything-goes channer culture. As charges of ethical lapses and corruption were thrown at the game journalists, accusations of death threats, sexual harassment, and doxxing were hurled right back at the gamers criticizing Depression Quest, its developer, and two notorious attention-seeking SJW fame whores who had quickly inserted themselves into the affair, shakedown artist Anita Sarkeesian and John Walker Flynt, a transvestite who calls himself "Brianna Wu". Collectively, the three SJWs became known among gamers as Literally Who, Literally Who 2, and Literally Wu as a means of safely referring to them without being accused of harassing them, as well as driving home the point that neither they nor their identities were relevant to the larger point of corruption in game journalism.

Being professional agitators, Literally Who 2 and Literally Wu soon came to dominate the media coverage, complete with fawning accounts of their courage featured everywhere from the *New York Times* to *Playboy* after they followed Literally Who's lead by claiming to have also been driven from their homes by similarly nonexistent death threats. Overshadowed by the two more dedicated drama queens, Literally Who gradually faded from the public eye while Literally Who 2 was later named one of *TIME Magazine*'s 100 Most Influential People in the World.

Things heated up rapidly in the second half of August 2014, as within a period of two weeks, 4chan purged the majority of its 45 moderators for being sympathetic to gamers, a dozen simultaneous "Gamers are Dead" articles were published on the same day by Ars Technica, Gamasutra, The Guardian, The Financial Post, Jezebel, and other sites, and actor Adam Baldwin of Firefly and The Last Ship fame tweeted a hashtag that would soon become feared and revered around the world.

#GAMERGATE was born.

I am an original GamerGater, which is to say that I am one of the gamers who was following the Internet Aristocrat and writing about corruption in game journalism related to The Zoe Post prior to Adam's famous tweet heard round the world. After being coined by Baldwin, the #GAMERGATE hashtag was tweeted 244,000 times in the first week alone, and since then has spawned everything from global gamer meetups to FBI investigations and an episode of Law & Order: Special Victims Unit. More importantly, the coalition of gamers that coalesced around #GAMERGATE has proven to be the first group to successfully drive back the SJWs assailing an industry, and for the first time, put the SJWs on the defensive. Where governments and militaries and corporations and church denominations and powerful organizations have failed to resist the SJWs for decades, a faceless group of loosely aligned gamers spanning the political spectrum has succeeded brilliantly. And in doing so, they have shown others, in other industries, how they can successfully strike back against the SJWs attacking them.

What caused such a broad and diverse group of gamers to come together, in my opinion, was the certain knowledge that there was a media conspiracy against them. This wasn't a mere sense of being under attack either, as we were in possession of absolute proof that a group of editors, reporters, and reviewers from various gaming news sites were using a private Google Groups mailing list called GameJournoPros to coordinate their vicious attacks on the gaming community and even the gamer identity itself. The story, broken on 17 September 2014 by British journalist Milo Yiannopoulos, was entitled "Exposed: The Secret Mailing List of the Gaming Journalism Elite" and confirmed the widespread impression many gamers had that they were being betrayed and besieged by the very gaming media that was supposed to serve them. Four days later, Milo published the complete list of all 137 individuals who belonged to the list.

The following anti-gamer articles were published in a three-day period between 28 August and 1 September, just after the christening of the anti-SJW gamer movement that would soon beat them into submission. While only one of the authors, Chris Plante of *Polygon*, was an actual member of the GameJournoPros mailing list, the combination of the seemingly coordinated attack and the evidence of the actual anti-gamer collusion was enough to harden most gamers' opinions about the complete lack of ethics in game journalism.

1. "'Gamers' don't have to be your audience. 'Gamers' are over." Leigh Alexander, *Gamasutra*

2. "An Awful Week to Care About Video Games", Chris Plante, *Polygon*

3. "A Guide to Ending 'Gamers', Devin Wilson," *Gamasutra*

4. "We Might be Witnessing the 'Death of an Identity'", Luke Plunkett, *Kotaku*

5. "Gaming is Leaving 'Gamers' Behind", Joseph Bernstein, *Buzzfeed*

6. "Sexism, Misogyny and Online Attacks: It's a Horrible Time to Consider Yourself a 'Gamer'", Patrick O'Rourke, *Financial Post*

7. "It's Dangerous to Go Alone: Why Are Gamers So Angry", Arthur Chu, *The Daily Beast*

8. "The End of Gamers", Dan Golding, *Tumblr*

9. "Misogynistic Trolls Drive Feminist Video Game Critic From Her Home", Callie Beusman, *Jezebel*

10. "A Disheartening Account Of The Harassment Going On In Gaming Right Now (And How Adam Baldwin Is Involved)", Victoria McNally, *The Mary Sue*

11. "Anita Sarkeesian Threatened with Rape and Murder for Daring to Keep Critiquing Video Games", Anna Minard, *Slog*

12. "Feminist Video Blogger Is Driven From Home by Death Threats", Jack Smith IV, *Betabeat*

13. "Fanboys, White Knights, and the Hairball of Online Misogyny", Tauriq Moosa, *The Daily Beast*

14. "The Death of 'Gamers' and the Women Who 'Killed' Them", Casey Johnston, *Ars Technica*

15. "The SJW effect—welcome to the end of the world", Patrick Garratt, *VG24/7*

16. "Announcement: Readers who feel threatened by equality no longer welcome", Tim Colwill, *GamesONnet*

17. "There are gamers at the gate, but they may already be dead", Jonathan Holmes, *Destructoid*

18. "This Week in Video Game Criticism: Tropes vs Anita Sarkeesian and the Demise of 'Gamers'", Kris Ligman, *Gamasutra*

19. "How to attack a woman who works in video gaming," Jenn Frank, the *Guardian*

The broad-based gamer response to this media onslaught was not organized in any way, and the tongue-in-cheek slogan "I am the Leader of #GAMER-GATE" beautifully expressed both its insouciance and its intrinsically ad hoc nature. It also reflected an instinctive awareness of the media SJWs' ability to target and destroy any individual who came to the fore; Adam Baldwin was attacked for being a celebrity sympathetic to the movement by a group of SJWs who put together a petition against his appearance as guest of honor to the Supanova Pop Culture Expo in Australia revoked and attempted to get his invitation revoked. They collected 6,305 signatures and an endorsement from Literally Wu, but their petition was declined by the expo's Founder and Event Director, rather more politely than their bullying behavior merited.

Indeed, the lack of a #GAMERGATE leader on whom they could focus their malicious attention greatly frustrated the SJWs, who, lacking any specific identity of their own, gradually became known as Anti-GamerGate, GamerGhazi, or AGGros. Various concern trolls repeatedly explained why #GAMERGATE needed a leader and how #GAMERGATE would never accomplish anything or be respected without a leader, concerns that were generally blown off with multiple GamerGaters declaring that they were the leader of #GAMERGATE or denouncing the concern troll as a shill, which is GG parlance for an individual who is not to be trusted. Within a month, the basic strategy of an entirely decentralized approach had come together; #Gamer-Gate had unwittingly reinvented a highly effective military strategy known as 4th Generation Warfare that has been driving professional warplanners mad since Vietnam.

The following quotations are selections from a highly influential document written by an anonymous GamerGater that effectively summarizes #GamerGate's successful anti-SJW approach. It was conceived as a comprehensive rebuttal to help GamerGaters address a specific type of shill known as The Changer.

> *All of the following are counterproductive and damage ourselves ONLY:*

No objectives, no goals, no demands, no philosophies, no lists.

- *It screws up the framing of the issue by forcing us to focus on specific issues.*
- *We do not need clear end points. If people are discouraged by a perceived lack of progress, take a break. This is an extended and long-term approach and you must take breaks. If you need specific goals for yourself, participate 2 or 3 days a week. Phrase it in those terms. Creating goals is not necessary.*

No narrative changing.

- *As we are a consumer revolt and not a political movement, we do not need a narrative.*
- *Narratives are for PR. PR is the journo's game. Not ours.*
- *We let the opposition change the narrative for themselves as they've done time and again for the last month.*
- *We are about facts, logic, and reason. A narrative is a way of spinning these. We have no spin. Only truth.*

No leaders.

- *This is a 100% shill idea put forward by the opposition to make it easy to play the identity game. This is their bread and butter and they will co-opt or ruin anything that they can get their hands on.*

- *There are currently no weak points to attack.*

- *As attacks against individuals intensify it's clear that giving them heads that are more important than others is a bad idea.*

Other shills to watch out for included The Fear Monger, The Defeatist, The Dismissive, The False Flag, The Politico, The Discreditor, The Misdirector, The Uncertain, The Slider, and The Self-Shiller; the document recommended specific responses to deal with each of them. This may strike you as paranoid, but I personally witnessed multiple shills of each of these types, as SJWs repeatedly tried to infiltrate and redirect what, despite outsiders' best efforts to categorize it as a hate group, a terrorist group, and a Twitter-based charade, remained a consumer revolt primarily against the corrupt games media.

The first #GamerGate ops were defensive in nature. #NotYourShield was the first big one and was designed to defang the SJW-pushed Narrative that #GamerGate was a collection of racist, sexist white males who were motivated by their hatred of women and minorities. The hashtag meant that the individual non-white, non-male GamerGater was refusing to grant Anti-GamerGate permission to use them as a shield to attack the white male members. The message was straight to the point: "The gaming community is diverse and strong. And we are #NotYourShield for the narrative you're creating." Thousands of GamerGaters, including Christina Hoff Sommers, a resident scholar at the American Enterprise Institute, Hispanic porn star Mercedes Carrera, black ex-game journalist Oliver Campbell, and yours truly, a Native American-Mexican game developer, utilized the hashtag and successfully destroyed that particular Narrative.

As A Girl in Vermilion succinctly put it, "We're all a motley crew of typically awesome people united by a common corruption". To demonstrate its lack of hostility to women, #GAMERGATE raised $10,000 for a female friend of a GamerGater who had been raped, $30,000 for the Honey Badger Brigade's legal fund after they were kicked out of the Calgary Comics Expo for publicly supporting #GAMERGATE, $17,000 for bullying prevention, $6,000 for suicide prevention, and $70,000 for a program designed to help women get into game development.

The SJWs, of course, clung stubbornly to their Narrative that #GAMERGATE hated women, despite the fact that most of the $133,000 raised was going directly to benefit human beings of the female persuasion and that the average male gamer has always been extremely enthusiastic about women who express even a modicum of interest in his hobby. All together now: SJWs always lie! The truth is that #GAMERGATE has always been a broad-based movement with three distinct aspects to it, as graphically demonstrated by an Italian GamerGater, Dr. Ethics.

While it was the most-tweeted op, #NOTYOURSHIELD was not the most effective of the various #GAMERGATE operations. Far and away the most successful was—is—Operation Disrespectful Nod. Unlike many of the other operations, it was a mailing campaign, not a hashtag or a fund-raising event, and also unlike most of the others, it was purely offensive in nature. Its purpose was to drain the financial lifeblood out of the gaming media sites that had declared war on gamers and #GAMERGATE. The initial targets were *Polygon*, *Gamasutra*, *Kotaku*, *Ars Technica*, *The Escapist*, *Rock Paper Shotgun*, and *Neogaf*; *The Escapist* was soon dropped from the list, however, as its editors covered #GAMERGATE much more fairly than the other sites and subsequently proceeded to disemploy a number of openly anti-#GAMERGATE contributors.

By the end of October 2014, Disrespectful Nod had already achieved enough success that the *Washington Post* wrote an article entitled "Inside

# WHAT IS #GAMERGATE?

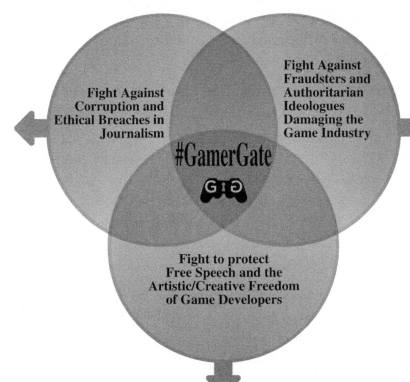

Gamergate's (successful) attack on the media".

> *Here, for the record, is how Gamergate does it—paraphrased from their own five-step war plans.*
>
> *Step 1: Consult Gamergate's compiled list of media organizations and reporters that have somehow wronged the movement. Once you have chosen the organization you would like to target, head over to the list of companies that advertise with that Web site and select one of them.*
>
> *Step 2: Consider the instance of "media malpractice" you plan to complain about. Other members of the movement have helpfully gathered examples already, as part of "Operation Dig Dig Dig": You might like to try the fact, for instance, that a gaming site reported on the harassment of game developer Zoe Quinn without acknowledging the remote possibility that Quinn may have made the whole thing up. Or you might flag the egregious "conflict of interest" between Quinn and the volunteer moderator of Reddit's gaming forum: said moderator is a friend of a co-worker of Quinn.*
>
> *Step 3: Choose an article on your targeted site to complain about or allege offense to. If no articles seem sufficiently offensive, comb through reporters' tweets for more material.*
>
> *Step 4: Plug all of your choices into one of the many form e-mails that leaders of Disrespectful Nod have helpfully written already.*
>
> *Step 5: Keep it up, even when you get no response, and be—to quote the operation's guide!—"an annoying little s–." A representative for a high-profile communications company that advertises on Polygon confirmed that he'd received "dozens" of e-mails from Gamergate supporters over a period of several weeks.*

*Operation Disrespectful Nod also encourages Gamergaters to reach out to the bosses and managers of journalists who have written "negative" stories, demanding the reporter in question be fired or asked to resign. Topping their most-wanted list, at present, is Gawker Media's Biddle.*

Two months later, Sam Biddle was forced to publicly apologize after *Gawker* lost more than one million dollars in advertising revenue due to Disrespectful Nod, and *Gawker* founder Nick Denton announced a management change. The Disrespectful Nod continued, and on July 20, 2015, both Tommy Craggs, the executive editor of *Gawker Media*, and Max Read, the editor-in-chief of Gawker.com, announced their resignations for reasons they claimed were related to their inability to "guarantee *Gawker*'s editorial integrity". Before the month had ended, five other *Gawker* employees followed them out the door, including features editor Leah Finnegan and senior editor Caity Weaver. And while Biddle is still there, the game journalist who claimed "nerds should be constantly shamed and degraded into submission" and called to "Bring Back Bullying" was shamed himself by hackers after he was exposed as having registered an account with the *Ashley Madison* adultery site.

As the owners of SJW-controlled media centers *Kotaku, Jezebel,* and *io9, Gawker* was #GamerGate's chief media target. But it was far from the only one. *Joystiq* was shut down in January 2015. In a textbook research operation, GamerGaters sleepax, Thurin, and br00ke27 took down an inept *InfoSec* contributor named Kim Crawley, who wrote an error-filled article without bothering to do any research but instead relied on nothing but openly anti-GamerGate sources. *Polygon*'s Ben Kuchera announced that he was "taking a break from gaming" that just happened to correspond with Emily Gera being let go at the same time while Movie Bob, who had angrily denounced #GamerGate as being the spiritual descendants of a group known for "violence, threats against children and racist rhetoric", was fired from *The Escapist*. Leigh Alexander, who helped launch the original "Gamers are Dead" attack, just happened to decide to leave *Gamasutra* to pursue exciting new opportunities around the same time.

No one knows exactly how much money #GAMERGATE has cost the game media that declared war on its own customers or precisely how many SJWs in the game journalist community are no longer with their previous employers as a result of Operation Disrespectful Nod. Both the journalism sites and the journalists themselves were desperate to avoid giving #GAMERGATE any readily confirmable trophies. But with the one-year anniversary of #GAMER-GATE approaching, no one would deny that #GAMERGATE has become a feared social media force, invoked in whispered tones at media companies, PR agencies, and publishing circles, and capable of taking over opposition hashtags and destroying SJW narratives at will. 43 #GGINX meetups have already taken place, from London and Paris to Sydney and Tel Aviv to Dallas, Los Angeles, and Washington, D.C. Vivian James, the #GAMERGATE mascot, is now a recognizable symbol around the world, and Vivian's striking green-and-purple ensemble has become a popular cosplayer costume at comic conventions.

#GAMERGATE is not going away anytime soon, and if anything, its numbers and its cultural influence are growing. Game devs, from small indie projects to giant AAA games, from unknowns to big names, are making it clear that they side with the gamers and not with the SJW game journos attempting to thought-police them.

*Game devs actually owe a tremendous debt to GamerGate, in my humble opinion. If GamerGate had not risen up, our creative freedom would be severely limited now. It's true. Gamers are the only ones who stopped SJWs and their crazy culture assault. Gamers conquer Dragons and fight Gods for a hobby.*

—Mark Kern, CEO, MEK Entertainment

The point at which it became obvious that #GamerGate had completely destroyed the SJW narrative was eleven months after Adam Baldwin gave it a name, when American conservatives suddenly began to develop a strange new respect for the very gamers that cultural conservatives had been periodically condemning since the *Dungeons & Dragons* scare of the Eighties. Conservative commentator Robert Stacy McCain wrote, "In war, your allies are whoever is fighting your enemies, and the motives of your allies matter far less than their skill in battle. Say what you will about #GamerGate, they are skilled and determined fighters. Operation Disrespectful Nod is making believers of anyone who ever made the mistake of underestimating them. Just ask Max Read."

Not only that, but outsiders began accusing both GamerGaters and high-profile #GamerGate allies such as Daryush Valizadeh and Mike Cernovich of "jumping on the #GamerGate bandwagon" in order to promote themselves. But ask yourself this: how stupid would a successful, self-promoting narcissist have to be in order to knowingly jump on the bandwagon of a much-vilified hate group of sexist, racist terrorists whose prime objective was to harass women and minorities? The combination of these two surprising developments made it evident to everyone that despite rolling out all the big guns of the cultural high ground they'd successfully infiltrated over the years, the SJW attempt to dictate a false Narrative about #GamerGate had failed.

Of course, this failure of the Narrative doesn't mean the media has given up gamedropping the dread hashtag at every opportunity. As per the Second Law, SJWs in the media continue to double down, again and again, and even after an entire year of spreading futile lies, they don't hesitate to make ever more nonsensical statements about the darkly exciting nemesis that stalks their vivid imaginations.

> *GamerGate makes a political movement out of threatening with*
> *rape any woman who has the temerity to offer an opinion about a*
> *videogame.*
>
> —Amy Wallace, *Wired*, 23 August 2015

Less than one year after Adam Baldwin coined the hashtag, #GAMERGATE had proven that a group of determined individuals could resist SJW attempts to enforce their thought policing in the game industry and even strike back at SJWs and SJW institutions to devastating effect. But could the lessons they'd learned be applied elsewhere, outside the game industry?

# Chapter 5

# RELEASE THE HOUNDS

*Brad, Larry, Vox—congratulations. You've spoiled the party. Not just mine, but everyone's. I waited nearly a half century to get here, and when I do get here, there's ashes. It hurts. Not just me. Everyone.*

—David Gerrold, science fiction author and SJW

In 2013, *New York Times* bestselling author Larry Correia was vexed. His *Monster Hunter International* books were a hit, and the books from his *Grimnoir* series were well-regarded and selling nicely, but he was often taunted by SJWs in science fiction for not being a real author. Although he'd been nominated for the John W. Campbell Award for Best New Writer in 2011, upon finding out that he was a conservative who wrote unabashed pulp fiction, the self-declared science fiction literati reacted rather like aristocrats discovering that a smelly peasant had been admitted to the ball. A European reviewer went so far as to declare, "If Larry Correia wins the Campbell, it will END LITERATURE FOREVER".

Furthermore, ever since the turn of the century, the works that had been winning the Hugo and Nebula awards were observably not the sort of works that had made the science fiction awards prestigious in the first place. In the place of *Dune* (Chilton), books like *The Quantum Rose*, Book 6 in The Saga of the Skolian Empire (Tor Books) were winning the Nebula. In the place of books like *Starship Troopers* (F&SF) and *A Canticle for Leibowitz* (J.B. Lippencott), we saw *Among Others* (Tor Books) and *Redshirts* (Tor Books) win the Hugo. Mediocre Tor-affiliated figures such as John Scalzi, Patrick Nielsen Hayden, and Charles Stross were collecting literally incredible numbers of nominations, more than legends of science fiction such as Isaac Asimov, Robert Heinlein, and Arthur C. Clarke ever did throughout their entire lifetimes. (As of 2015, the current count is 39 nominations for the three Torlocks mentioned versus 31 for the three deceased SF legends.) It had become obvious to even the most casual observer that the once-prestigious science fiction awards had become little more than a popularity contest dominated by a small group of writers, most of whom were affiliated with science fiction's largest publisher, Tor Books, the home of the very SF literati that sneered at Larry Correia.

The extent to which the SJW-run Tor Books has dominated the science fiction awards for the last three decades can hardly be exaggerated. Tor has won the Locus Award for Best Publisher for the last 27 years in a row. Since 1986, 46 of the 190 novels nominated for Hugo Awards and 38 of the 156 novels nominated for the Nebula Award have been published by Tor. Nor is it a coincidence that the number of award-winning books that the science fiction public does not read has also increased dramatically during this time. The average current Amazon rank for the three pre-Tor award-winners—the newest having won in 1966—is 3,685. The average Amazon rank for the three most recent Tor award-winners—the oldest having won in 2002—is 665,597.

It is worth noting that there is a clear connection between this recent domination of the awards by SJWs and the politics of the writers. Hugo Awards historian Mike Glynn estimates that in the last 20 years, across all the various categories, conservative SF authors and editors have won a grand total of 19 out of a possible 266 Hugo Awards.

Not only that, but the dominance of Tor Books came about at the same time as the infestation of the editorial positions at the major science fiction publishers by SJWs, most of them female, who promptly began an aggressive gatekeeping campaign to publish more diverse and female authors while systematically eradicating what they considered to be the offensive and problematic elements rife within classic science fiction and fantasy. One SJW aptly expressed their collective hatred for the very literary genre they had taken over when she wrote about reading National Public Radio's list of the 100 greatest science fiction and fantasy novels.

> *I devoured science fiction and fantasy when I was younger—the idea that I was also devouring patriarchal and sexist ideas made me deeply uncomfortable… The fact that these were all supposed to be the best of the genre, was even more shocking. I can understand how many of the books on the list may have once been groundbreaking but that doesn't mean that they are now the best examples of the genre. They have been supplanted, hundreds of times over, by other authors that took similar themes but made them better and more inclusive.*

> —"I read the 100 'best' fantasy and sci-fi novels—and they were shockingly offensive", Liz Lutgendorff, *New Statesman*

Of course, the general science fiction public tended to disagree; according to *Publishers Weekly*, science fiction sales are down more than 50 percent since 2008. As the SJWs at the science fiction publishers continue to sign and publish these "better and more inclusive" books, science fiction readers tend to continue buying the older books and ignoring the new ones. But old books can't win new awards, and the awards were going to novels and shorter works that had no chance of standing the test of time. Indeed, many of them have already been forgotten less than a decade after first being published.

To prove the once-prestigious Hugo Awards were now little more than a popularity contest dominated by a small left-wing cabal, Larry Correia launched his Campaign to End Puppy-Related Sadness caused by boring SJW message fiction in 2013. More commonly known by the name Sad Puppies, the campaign was modestly successful, and although Correia himself didn't make the Hugo shortlist in the Best Novel category, he drummed up enough support among his readers to get several works by other authors nominated in some of the lesser categories. The next year, as part of his new campaign entitled *Sad Puppies 2: Rainbow Puppy Lighthouse, The Huggening*, he nominated my novelette "Opera Vita Aeterna", in part because he liked it, but also, as he remarked, because the Devil didn't have anything eligible in 2014. He explained his reasoning as follows at *Monster Hunter Nation*, his blog named after his bestselling exurban fantasy gun porn series.

> *1. I said a chunk of the Hugo voters are biased toward the left, and put the author's politics far ahead of the quality of the work. Those openly on the right are sabotaged. This was denied.*
>
> *2. So I got some right wingers on the ballot.*
>
> *3. The biased voters immediately got all outraged and mobilized to do exactly what I said they'd do.*
>
> *4. Point made.*
>
> *For the record, I'm only the second most hated man who got a nomination. The most despised is Vox Day by far, however, I'm the one who suggested him to my fans who were participating in Sad Puppies 2. So if he's their devil, I'm the antichrist.*

As anticipated, the Sad Puppies' nominees were destroyed in the shortlist voting that year. The Hugos have a peculiar and rather complicated voting system, so Larry's *Warbound* finished fourth in the first-preference voting, but fifth out of the five novels nominated after all was said and done. "Opera

Vita Aeterna" did even worse, actually finishing sixth out of five, and behind No Award. This turned out to be useful information for us, as by comparing the results with some of the other Puppy candidates, it allowed us to distinguish between the general anti-Puppy vote, the anti-Larry vote, and the anti-Vox vote. The anti-Puppy vote, which indicated the core SJW vote, was about 600, while the anti-Larry vote was 900 and the anti-Vox vote was 1,100, thereby confirming who the SJWs in science fiction hated the most.

The SJWs celebrated, of course, and indulged in their usual Narrative-spinning, crowing about how upset the Sad Puppies were now that we had learned our bitter lesson. That might have been the end of the story, except they made one fatal mistake. Both Sad Puppies 1 and Sad Puppies 2 were Correia's campaigns. I wasn't involved in them at all, except as one of a number of authors whose works he had recommended. Incredibly, my complete lack of involvement in both campaigns somehow didn't prevent the SJWs from accusing me of gaming the award.

Now, I am a professional game designer. If I am going to game an award, it certainly isn't going to be to obtain one nomination in a minor category for myself. As it happens, I don't care about awards. I'm just not wired that way. Perhaps I'm too arrogant or too elitist to care about awards, (all right, I'm probably too arrogant and too elitist), but regardless, awards have simply never been of interest to me. I've been nominated for a few awards here and there, and my band Psykosonik even beat out Prince for Best Dance Record back in the Nineties, but I've never attended a single awards ceremony for either music or literature.

I didn't mind finishing 6th out of 5. In fact, I thought it was rather funny and proudly adopted Six of Five as my Borg name. But to be accused of gaming an award in such an inept manner was, to me, an insult not to be borne. So, rather than leaving the whole burden on Larry Correia's giant shoulders for a third year (in case you weren't aware, Larry does not look like your typical creepy SF author, but can be not unreasonably described as a six-foot-five bearded Murder Hobo), the Evil Legion of Evil, a group of loosely affiliated science fiction and fantasy writers of varying degrees of success, joined forces for the Sad Puppies 3 campaign. I believe I still have the notes of the first meeting of the Legion, which took place on January 16, 2015.

VOX DAY, SUPREME DARK LORD: Welcome, my black knights, my devious and subtle dark ladies. The circle is joined. Tell me, what evil hath thou wrought?

TOM KRATMAN: GRAND STRATEGIKON: Sir! Another 64 crossbeams, 97 posts, and 468 iron nails have been prepared and added to the warehouse, sir! Four more excruciators have been trained and are good to go, sir!

LARRY CORREIA, INTERNATIONAL LORD OF HATE: Bloody hell, Tom! How many crosses do you think we need? We haven't even crucified *anyone* yet!

KRATMAN: I just like to be prepaaaaared, sir!

DAY: So how many pinkshirts can we crucify? Give me a daily average.

KRATMAN: All of them!

SARAH HOYT, BEAUTIFUL BUT EVIL SPACE PRINCESS: All of them?

KRATMAN: All of them! We're cocked, locked, and ready to rock!

HOYT (whispers to Correia): Kate's going to be pissed. She had her heart set on impaling McCreepy. [McCreepy is how we refer to an SJW and Torlock named Jim C. Hines. Let's just say you wouldn't allow him anywhere near your children if you saw him lurking around the playground. Kate the Impaler is Kate

Paulk, the Evil Legion of Evil member who will be spearheading Sad Puppies 4.]

Day: Stand down, Tom. Good work. Anyone else?

John Wright, Living Brain, King in Yellow, and Speaker to Morlocks: I have erected, at great personal expense, a 91-foot-tall idol of radioactive black marble to your likeness in the caves of Logan County, West Virginia, where I and a coterie of degenerate hillbillies, drug-maddened Saponi and Shawnee shamen, and blood-drinking devil dogs, together with an inhuman living fungus from Pluto, make hideous sacrifices and perform acts of unspeakable abomination to adore our idol of Vox Day, impiously dreaming of the return of the Elder Stargods from Hyades in Taurus. For we adore Vox Day! Crowned with Five Divine Cobras of Might, His Buttocks Sit Atop the Thunder-Winged Garuda Bird!

Day: All I asked for was the latest draft of *Somewhither*, John.

Wright: Oh, yes. Let me see. Ah, here it is.

Brad Torgersen, Soft and Cuddly Token Liberal: Hey, Larry, what's this?

Correia: Dammit, Brad, put down–

Torgersen: ah ha ha ha ha ha!

Correia: …the flamethrower…

The original plan was for Sarah Hoyt to take the lead on Sad Puppies 3, but when she fell ill, the Legion's token liberal, Brad Torgersen, took over for her as the standard-bearer. While Brad and I get along just fine, he's a liberal (although not an SJW), and a fair number of his friends were less than entirely comfortable finding themselves affiliated with the Lord Voldemort of science fiction. In a reflection of the divide in #GamerGate between the

GGers focused solely on ethics in game journalism and those more interested in fighting SJWs, it soon became clear that we had different objectives. Larry Correia's goal was to expose the left-wing bias in the system, and he had already succeeded beautifully. Brad's admirable goal, which was considerably more ambitious, and in my opinion, highly unlikely, was to save science fiction from the SJWs who had infested it. As for me, I thought we should just blow up what had become little more than an SJW institution and public relations tool and start over. To put these goals in practical terms, Brad wanted to actually try to win awards for what he deemed to be meritorious work, whereas I thought we ought to nominate whatever would most upset the SJWs and then turn around and join them in voting No Award for everything in order to leave a smoking hole where the 2015 Hugos had been.

Architects versus arsonists, one might say.

After discussing our differences, I stepped back from Sad Puppies and created Rabid Puppies, an allied campaign designed around the #GAMER-GATE model. It was enthusiastically embraced by the Dread Ilk of *Vox Popoli*, the larger of my two blogs, and as was the case with #GAMERGATE, the anti-SJW people proved to be more numerous than those focused only on the industry-specific issue. However, the SJWs so hated everything Brad put forward, and reacted so negatively towards those works, that instead of needing a completely separate list of recommendations, the Rabid Puppy list turned out to be little more than the Sad Puppy list with a few tactical additions intended to further enrage the SJWs.

To describe the Sad Puppies 3 campaign as successful would be a massive understatement. The Puppies essentially swept the awards between them, and we could have easily taken every single nomination if we'd wanted to bother doing so. SJWs in science fiction, such as George R.R. Martin, the author of *A Game of Thrones*, were astonished to discover that their little cabal of Torlocks had been prevented from dominating the awards for the first time in two decades. Of course, this failure to collect their customary award-tribute was taken as a sign that the awards had been irretrievably broken.

> *"Call it block voting. Call it ballot stuffing. Call it gaming the system. There's truth to all of those characterisations. You can't call it cheating, though. It was all within the rules. But many things can be legal, and still bad…and this is one of those, from where I sit. I think the Sad Puppies have broken the Hugo awards, and I am not sure they can ever be repaired," he wrote.*

—Alison Flood, "George RR Martin says rightwing lobby has 'broken' Hugo awards", the *Guardian*, April 9, 2015

While both Puppy campaigns were conducted completely within the rules, there was no truth to Martin's claims of bloc-voting, much less ballot-stuffing. In fact, there was considerably more statistical variance across the pro-Puppy votes than there had been across the votes from the historical Tor-led voting bloc. As the SF awards analyst, Brendan Kempner of *Chaos Horizon,* correctly noted, the difference between the 368 nominations for the top Editor Long Form nominee and the mere 230 for the lead Short Story candidate when both categories were Puppy-swept meant that that "not every Puppy voter was a straight slate voter."

All we had really done was to show up and vote in unexpected numbers. As a result, between Sad Puppies and Rabid Puppies, we took 61 out of the original 85 shortlist nominations, including a pair for me as Best Editor, Short Form, and Best Editor, Long Form. John C. Wright received a record-setting six nominations (one of which was later disqualified for spurious reasons), LTC Tom Kratman, the former U.S. Army Ranger who is the only author more hated and feared by SJWs than I am, was nominated for Best Novella, and Larry Correia was nominated for Best Novel. Correia, whose primary goal had always been to prove his point about the awards being left-wing popularity contests, declined the nomination, prompting this hilarious exchange between him and SJW author John Scalzi, whose Tor-published novel *Lock In* had been widely predicted to bring him his 10th Hugo nomination in 2015.

> *John Scalzi @scalzi*
>
> *I wish Larry Corriea had the balls to admit the reason he started the Sad Puppies campaign was that he just wanted a Hugo so fucking bad.*
>
> *45 retweets 66 favorites*

> *Larry Correia @monsterhunter45*
>
> *I turned down my Hugo nomination and you still didn't make the ballot.*
>
> *360 retweets 501 favorites*

See: The Third Law of SJW. *SJWs always project.*

It was fascinating, and more than a little amusing, to witness the shock and horror of science fiction's SJWs, who simply could not believe that a group of anti-SJW revolutionaries could so effortlessly *obliterate* their cherished awards. They promptly resorted to the usual SJW tactic of attempting to reframe the Narrative through media spin, calling in favors and unconsciously imitating the actions of the GameJournoPros from the year before by planting identical stories, using identical terminology, not only in the usual pro-SJW publications like *Gawker* and the *Guardian*, but everywhere from *National Public Radio* and *Popular Science* to the *New Zealand Herald* and the *Wall Street Journal.* Because they found it impossible to believe that we had so much more popular support than they did, they actually blamed #GAMERGATE for their humiliating defeat. However, the truth is that there were only two GamerGaters involved in Rabid Puppies, Daddy Warpig and me, and none at all in Sad Puppies.

The Toad of Tor, aka former Tor contributing editor Teresa Nielsen Hayden, was apoplectic and even more obnoxious than usual.

> *"Why are people talking about what would happen if everyone who reads SF voted in the Hugos? IMO, it's not a relevant question. The Hugos don't belong to the set of all people who read the genre; they belong to the worldcon, and the people who attend and/or support it. The set of all people who read SF can start their own award…I know what they're doing. I want the Justice Department to declare [#GamerGate] a criminal organization and hit them with felony charges. It would not be an excessive response to their actions. These are the people the Sad Puppies have invited into our annual gathering."*

Needless to say, she was promptly crucified on her own words, which helped bring the anti-SJW battle in science fiction to #GamerGate's attention. If #GamerGate hadn't been sympathetic to the Sad Puppies before, they certainly were after being attacked by SJWs again for something they hadn't done. Popular #GamerGate artist Kukuruyo created an image that represented the way many GamerGaters had come to feel; #GamerGate and Sad

Vivian James

Puppies might not be the same, but since they shared the same SJW enemy, they were destined to be friends and allies.

Another popular #GAMERGATE cartoon showed GG icon Vivian James petting a puppy and saying, "I don't know why everyone says you're my dog, but you sure are cute". Even so, the Toad of Tor's hopping-mad rants calling for federal action to intervene and defend Tor's Gaia-given right to win SF awards weren't the most insane reaction. *Entertainment Weekly* published a hit piece that was so outrageous that the editors had to revise it twice before issuing a correction that still didn't cover all of the mischaracterizations and lies. The excised portions from the original piece are indicated by strike-through.

~~Hugo Award nominations fall victim to misogynistic, racist voting campaign~~

Correction: Hugo Awards voting campaign sparks controversy

by Isabella Biedenharn

CORRECTION: *After misinterpreting reports in other news publications, EW published an unfair and inaccurate depiction of the Sad Puppies voting slate, which does, in fact, include many women and writers of color. As Sad Puppies' Brad Torgerson explained to EW, the slate includes both women and non-caucasian writers, including Rajnar Vajra, Larry Correia, Annie Bellet, Kary English, Toni Weisskopf, Ann Sowards, Megan Gray, Sheila Gilbert, Jennifer Brozek, Cedar Sanderson, and Amanda Green.*

*This story has been updated to more accurately reflect this. EW regrets the error.*

~~The Hugo Awards have fallen victim to a campaign in which misogynist groups lobbied to nominate only white males for the science fiction book awards. These groups, Sad Puppies~~

~~and Rabid Puppies (both of which are affiliated with last year's~~
~~GamerGate scandal), urged sci-fi fans to become members~~
~~of the Hugo Awards' voting body, World Science Fiction~~
~~Convention, in order to cast votes against female writers and~~
~~writers of color.   Membership only costs $40, and allows~~
~~members to vote for the 2016 nominations as well as the 2015~~
~~nominations, which were just released.~~

Many science fiction writers are up in arms with a slate of Hugo Awards nominees lobbied by two groups affiliated with last year's GamerGate scandal, Sad Puppies and Rabid Puppies.

Sad Puppies broadcast their selection on Feb. 1, writing: "If you agree with our slate below—and we suspect you might—this is YOUR chance to make sure YOUR voice is heard." Brad Torgerson, who runs Sad Puppies along with Larry Correia, complains that the Hugo Awards have lately skewed toward "literary" works, as opposed to "entertainment".

Torgerson also writes that he disagrees with Hugos being awarded for affirmative action-like purposes, as many women and writers of color went home with awards in 2014: "Likewise, we've seen the Hugo voting skew ideological, as Worldcon and fandom alike have tended to use the Hugos as an affirmative action award: giving Hugos because a writer or artist is (insert underrepresented minority or victim group here) or because a given work features (insert underrepresented minority or victim group here) characters."

The other lobbying group, Rabid Puppies, is run by Vox Day. As *The Telegraph* reports, "Members of the Science Fiction and Fantasy Writers of America have called for Beale's exclusion from the group after he has written against women's suffrage and posted racist views towards black writer NK Jemisin."

~~Fortunately, some sane voters allowed well-deserving writers to pull through. Ann Leckie's Ancillary Sword and Listen was nominated for Dramatic Presentation, and Annie Bellet's Goodnight Stars was nominated, despite having a non-white, female protagonist.~~

~~Plenty of members of the science fiction community have voiced their disgust with both sects of "Puppies."~~ Writer Philip Sandifer wrote on his blog Sunday, "The Hugo Awards have just been successfully hijacked by neofascists." Sandifer's post, which is worth reading in full, addresses what this disaster means for the sci-fi world:

"To be frank, it means that traditional sci-fi/fantasy fandom does not have any legitimacy right now. Period. A community that can be this effectively controlled by someone who thinks black people are subhuman and who has called for acid attacks on feminists is not one whose awards have any sort of cultural validity. That sort of thing doesn't happen to functional communities. And the fact that it has just happened to the oldest and most venerable award in the sci-fi/fantasy community makes it unambiguously clear that traditional sci-fi/fantasy fandom is not fit for purpose."

Sandifer's libelous assertions had virtually nothing to do with reality, but he was right in one regard. The Puppies had shown the world that science fiction was no longer fit for the purpose of cramming SJW ideology down the throats of unsuspecting readers.

One fascinating thing about the SJW-driven coverage of the upheaval in the Hugo Awards, which drew more media attention than the awards had received in the last ten years combined, was the fact that even though

Rabid Puppies was widely recognized to have been the driving force behind the incredible success of the Puppies, no one except Michael Rapoport of the *Wall Street Journal* ever talked to any of us about it. They interviewed George R. R. Martin, they interviewed John Scalzi, they quoted literary irrelevancies like Philip Sandifer, and a few of them even talked to Brad Torgersen, but they did not talk to me or any of the other Rabid Puppies.

Of course, by now you probably understand why they didn't. It's a lot harder to sell a false narrative about someone when they are able to speak directly for themselves. It was more useful for the SJW Narrative to quote someone I'd never met who was willing to lie about what I think—I don't think black people are subhuman—and willing to lie about what I have done—I have never called for acid attacks, on feminists or on anyone else—than to permit me to accurately represent my views, however controversial they may be. Because, as you will recall from Chapter Two, the primary objective of the SJW is always to destroy, discredit, and disqualify any individual who threatens the Narrative.

The problem for the media, and for the science fiction SJWs who were hoping to wield it as a weapon, is that the Internet prevents them from being able to control and dictate the Narrative the way they could in the pre-Internet era. It permits those being assailed by SJWs to take the social pressure being brought to bear against them and, as with jujitsu, use that very pressure against them. For example, when the Creative Director of Tor Books and Associate Publisher of TOR.COM, Irene Gallo, made the mistake of repeating the same false Narrative the media had been pushing on her personal Facebook page, we were able to use it against her by extensively quoting it, comparing her words to the corporate Code of Conduct which they violated, and demanding her resignation.

*There are two extreme right-wing to neo-nazi groups, called the Sad Puppies and the Rabid Puppies respectively, that are calling for the end of social justice in science fiction and fantasy. They*

*are unrepentantly racist, sexist and homophobic. A noisy few but*
*they've been able to gather some Gamergate folks around them and*
*elect a slate of bad-to-reprehensible works on this year's Hugo ballot.*

Now, one might have thought Tor Books would immediately fire an employee who not only attacked the publisher's customers but also its own authors and books—several of those "bad-to-reprehensible works" were written by longtime Tor authors Kevin J. Anderson and John C. Wright, and one of the novels nominated by the Puppies had even been published by Tor—but what would have gotten a minimum-wage employee fired at McDonald's or Walmart only resulted in a non-apology and a mild public reprimand from the SJW-dominated publisher.

This shows why simply turning the SJW attack sequence around on SJWs tends to be less effective for normal people than it is for SJWs using it against them; the key to Stage Six is that the Authority to whom one is Appealing be Amenable. While SJWs are always loyal to other SJWs first, normal people have an instinctive tendency to defend fellow employees or members of the group regardless of whether they are SJWs or not and may even resent what they see as an outside attempt to interfere with their business. Unlike the cases of Sir Tim Hunt and John Derbyshire, the management at Macmillan, the corporate owner of Tor Books, was not eager to jettison the targeted employee because doing so would not please SJWs in the media.

However, as #GAMERGATE has shown, that doesn't mean they won't oust her eventually. It merely means more pressure is required. To date, over two thousand emails have been sent to Macmillan demanding Gallo's resignation, and more than 500 former customers are participating in a boycott of Tor Books that will not end until Irene Gallo has been held responsible for her unprofessional, code of conduct-violating comments by the termination of her employment. But regardless of how that particular matter turns out, an important battle has already been won, as the publishing gatekeepers at Tor

Books have had their public bully pulpit, from which they preached SJW sermons and denounced violators of their science fiction Narrative for more than 20 years, forcibly removed from them once and for all by their unhappy corporate masters.

The importance of Sad Puppies is that it shows how even in a field that has been dominated by SJWs for more than two decades, they are weaker and less numerous than most people believe. Not only are they far from invulnerable, even in the fields they observably control, but it may be that only two or three men willing to resist them are required in order to explode their Narrative.

This is not to say that even in a field as small as science fiction, the cultural war can be won overnight. On August 22nd, the 2015 Hugo Awards were presented. Desperate to deny the Sad Puppies a victory, the SJWs resorted to scorched earth tactics to deny awards to the best-selling Jim Butcher, long-time Baen Books editor Toni Weisskopf, science fiction grandmaster John C. Wright, and even 5-time winner and 38-time nominee Mike Resnick, voting all of them below No Award. For the first time in 72 years, no awards were given out in five categories, including Best Novella, Best Short Story, Best Related Work, Best Editor (Long Form), and Best Editor (Short Form). While this was a disappointment to the Sad Puppies, it was no surprise to the Rabids, as my plan from the start had been based on the correct premise that the SJWs would rather destroy the awards than lose control of them.

And while we didn't have the numbers to force through a No Award vote on our own, we were able to get them to do it for us by nominating works by authors, editors, and publishers they hated. We also managed to tip the scale and ensure that Cixin Liu's hard science fiction novel, *The Three-Body Problem*, won Best Novel over Katherine Addison's tedious SJW angst-fest, *The Goblin Emperor*. Unsurprisingly, this didn't prevent the SJWs from declaring victory. 15-time Hugo nominee Charles Stross's take on the matter summed up the SJW position nicely: "Fans 5, Puppies 0. Club members kick gatecrashers out the door."

In doing so, Stross underlined a point Brad Torgersen had previously made about the Sad Puppies being seen as wrongfans engaged in badthink reading wrongbooks. The SJWs tried to insist that our post-award celebrations were merely attempts to salvage wounded pride, but the Puppies, both Sad and Rabid, knew better. Unbeknownst to most SJWs, Larry Correia had let the cat out of the bag four months before in a public exchange with George Martin on *Monster Hunter Nation*.

> *Vox is off doing his own thing. You tried to shun a man who is incapable of being shunned. He got kicked out of the market, so went and built his own market. The more you go after him, the stronger he gets. I don't think you guys realize that most of me and Brad's communication with Vox consists of us asking him to be nice and not burn it all down.*
>
> —"George R. R. Martin Responds", Larry Correia,
> April 14, 2015

We didn't burn it all down, but nuking five out of sixteen categories wasn't a bad start. After only three years of Puppy-related insurgencies, the SJWs have already thrown in the towel and begun changing the rules. In doing so, they have abandoned all hope of retaining their previous control over the Hugo Awards in the future despite having outnumbered us two-to-one across the board in 2015. (In the Best Editor category, No Award beat Toni Weisskopf 2,496 to 1,216, while in the Novella category, the vote was 3,495 for No Award versus 1,832 first-preference votes for all the various Puppy-nominated novellas combined.)

At the business meeting the day after the awards, a group of SJWs successfully championed the adoption of no less than three new rules to govern the nominations, most notably a complicated one called E Pluribus Hugo.

If ratified at MidAmeriCon next year, it will transform the Hugo Awards into a quasi-Parliamentary system designed to ensure no single faction can singlehandedly dictate the shortlist in the future. This will have the effect of preventing future Puppy sweeps but will also limit the Tor cabal to one or two nominations per category as well. And since our goal was never to control the awards, but merely to break the SJW stranglehold on them, this will be an eminently satisfactory outcome from the canine perspective.

But there is a broader lesson here that goes well beyond the weird little world of science fiction. The lesson of the 2015 Hugo Awards is this: SJWs care so much about the institutions they control that they will destroy them rather than relinquish control over them.

# Chapter 6

# THE SJW NEXT DOOR

*You belong to your father, the devil, and you want to carry out your*
*father's desires. He was a murderer from the beginning, not holding*
*to the truth, for there is no truth in him. When he lies, he speaks*
*his native language, for he is a liar and the father of lies.*

—John 8:44

If you are a normal person reading this, someone who isn't an ideological extremist or a political radical, but a regular guy working IT at a mid-sized corporation or a regular woman working in a retail establishment downtown, it might strike you that SJWs are only a problem in the alien worlds of the game industry or science fiction publishing. You may well believe equality is a good thing, diversity is a strength, and while you're not necessarily enthusiastic about the sudden influx of foreign immigrants speaking alien languages in your town, you're trying to be open-minded about it. After all, your great-great-grandparents were immigrants too, and America is the great melting pot.

And if it seems a little crazy that men can legally marry men now, or you occasionally wonder why, if "Caitlyn Jenner" is really a woman, Wikipedia says she is known for winning the men's decathlon at the 1976 Summer

Olympics, none of that is anything that has much to do with your day-to-day life. Sure, the directives that occasionally show up in your inbox from HR are increasingly bizarre, and neither you nor anyone else in your department knew what to make of the most recent mandatory harassment seminar, which involved four hours of listening to an individual of uncertain sex wearing a dress and alternating between shouting at everyone and bursting into tears, but it turned out to be a real team-building experience and even provided everyone with a few new office catchphrases.

So even though you can see how SJWs may cause problems elsewhere, for other people, you can't see how it is any real concern of yours. And that complacency is the chief ingredient in the long-term success SJWs have enjoyed in gradually taking the cultural high ground.

SJWs don't begin by storming an institution en masse, breaking down the doors, and sacrificing the secretary in the lobby to Satan before defecating on the carpets and copulating madly on the table in the meeting room. SJWs enter by stealth, using mousy middle-aged women and little inoffensive men to whom no one could possibly object. They are outwardly good-natured individuals who tend to keep their political opinions to themselves and rapidly make themselves indispensable to the people in charge. They tend to gravitate towards positions of influence rather than authority and towards internally-focused objectives that are hard to measure rather than externally-focused responsibilities where success or failure are obvious. In the corporate context, Human Resources is their natural habitat; they're also often found in Marketing or as much-appreciated assistants to the executives.

They work hard, they don't complain, and most of their colleagues would find it difficult to even begin to describe what their politics might be. Their loyalties appear to lie primarily with the organization. Indeed, they are often among its foremost defenders and champions. Think about the little old lady who helps out at church, the mother who always makes cookies and bars for the Boy Scout troop, the married forty-something man without kids who is the obvious choice for the homeowners association board, and the young man who is always able to find the spare time to drive a carful of teenagers to the youth camp on the weekend.

Whenever something needs to be done, they're usually the first to volunteer. So it's hardly surprising that it seldom takes long before they are in positions of influence where their opinions are not only taken seriously but actively sought out. And that's when they can start planting the seeds for taking over the organization.

SJW entryists have two primary objectives. The first is to bring more SJWs into the organization. Sometimes it is blatant, such as when a large public corporation's first female board member predictably declares that the organization's priority should be hiring more women. More often it is subtle, like when there is a vacancy and the stealth SJW notes that he just happens to know someone who would be perfect for the job, even if that person doesn't appear to have any of the relevant skills required for it. He will almost certainly have the qualifications, though. SJWs absolutely love qualifications, as they are easy to understand and provide an easy excuse for weeding out any problematic applicants who look as if they might threaten the Narrative.

The second entryist objective is to establish a code of conduct. This is an old bait-and-switch that has been used on everyone from the Go Programming Language community to British Prime Minister Margaret Thatcher by the advocates of the European Union. What happens is that the SJW proposes a code of conduct, explaining that due to the way in which the corporation or church or community is growing, it is now necessary to formalize and structure its rules. After making allusions to a few differences of opinion that have taken place in the past and expressing concerns about hypothetical future problems, the SJW asserts the need for some behavioral guidelines, but guidelines are goal-oriented suggestions rather than specific hard-and-fast rules.

*"We had to learn the hard way that by agreement to what were apparently empty generalizations or vague aspirations we were later held to have committed ourselves to political structures which were contrary to our interests."*

—Lady Margaret Thatcher, *The Downing Street Years*

To understand how intentionally vague aspirations are transformed into firm political structures that are used to control institutions and entire communities, consider the example of the Go community. Go is a programming language developed at Google and launched in 2007. The Go programmers call themselves "gophers", and they have an official mailing list called golang-nuts as well as an annual conference called Gophercon.

As you might expect, the gophers are infested with a number of SJWs who are militantly pro-women-in-tech, who believe the heavily male demographics of the community are a serious problem in need of a solution, and who have put themselves in positions of influence where they can transform their SJW priorities into the priorities of the entire community. Consider this email from an SJW gopher who unilaterally decided that the gopher community required thought-policing.

*Since Go was launched nearly six years ago, our community has grown from a small group of enthusiasts to thousands of programmers from all corners of the globe. I am proud of us; so many great projects and such a helpful and passionate group of people. Sincerely, I consider myself lucky to be involved.*

*But as we grow we should reflect on how we can improve.*

*Take this mailing list, for example. While the majority of discussions here are respectful and polite, occasionally they take a turn for the worse. While such incidents are rare, they are noticeable and have an effect on the tone of other discussions. We can do better.*

*At times we can be overly didactic, meeting opposing ideas with inflexibility. When challenged by a differing opinion we should not be defensive, but rather take the opportunity to discuss and debate so that we may better understand our own ideas.*

*I'm also concerned by reports of abuse, harassment, and discrimination in our community, particularly toward women and other underrepresented groups. Even I have experienced harassment and abuse myself. This may be common in the tech industry but it is not OK.*

*We are the Go community; we get to choose what is OK and what is not. It's not a choice but a responsibility, and it is a responsibility that we have neglected too long.*

*The positive effects of diversity in communities are well-documented. If our community is to continue to grow and prosper, we must make it a more inclusive place, where all are respected and nobody is made to feel dismissed, unwelcome, or unsafe.*

*To that end, I propose that we establish a Code of Conduct that would cover the behavior of community members on the various Go mailing lists and the golang subreddit, on IRC, in private Go-related correspondence, and at Go events.*

*I believe that any Code of Conduct we adopt should be goal-oriented ("this is what we aspire to") rather than rules-oriented ("don't do this!"). I also believe it should empower the community to help maintain a high standard: I want everyone to feel comfortable calling out bad behavior, without the need to appeal to authority.*

*I have done a survey of similar codes in various communities and the Django Code of Conduct is the one I like best. I am in favor of basing our code directly on that document.*

One didn't need to know anything about the individual to know that this was a classic, indeed, almost textbook example of an SJW attempting to make the transformation from entryism to community control. Consider the tell-tale phrases and what they really mean:

- *"As we grow we should reflect on how we can improve."* This organization is relevant enough to be worth controlling.

- *"We can do better."* It is time to stamp out badthink and to expel anyone who challenges the Narrative.

- *"Take the opportunity to discuss and debate."* Shut up and accept the dictates of your moral superiors.

- *"I'm also concerned by reports of abuse, harassment, and discrimination in our community, particularly toward women and other underrepresented groups."* Please note that I am now applying the Narrative to our community. The fact that these reports are entirely fictional is irrelevant.

- *"We get to choose what is OK and what is not."* We SJWs will inform you what is acceptable and what is not. Don't be mistaken and think that your opinion is either desired or relevant here.

- *"The positive effects of diversity in communities are well-documented."* I am perfectly willing to lie and say anything that will support the Narrative. (The fact is that diversity destroys communities by weakening trust, and reducing social capital and engagement levels within them. See Robert Putnam, "E Pluribus Unum: Diversity and Community in the Twenty-first Century".)

- *"Nobody is made to feel dismissed, unwelcome, or unsafe."* If you dare to criticize the irrelevant ideas of women who don't actually do anything in the project, you are the problem, and you will pay for it.

- *"I propose that we establish a Code of Conduct."* I propose that we establish a thought-and-speech Gestapo who will police the community in order to identify and eliminate any crimethinkers who challenge the Narrative.

- *"Any Code of Conduct we adopt should be goal-oriented ('this is what we aspire to') rather than rules-oriented ('don't do this!')."* We prefer nebulousness and flexibility to specifying actual rules in order to prevent crimethinkers from avoiding punishment by challenging the Narrative without breaking any rules. (SJWs always resist any attempt to identify or codify specifics in order to avoid being held accountable to the rules they apply to their targets.)

- *"I have done a survey of similar codes in various communities."* This has worked for SJWs who have taken control of other communities, so there is no reason it won't work here.

After six days of what passed for discussion between a grand total of 104 gophers out of the "thousands of programmers" in the community, without any vote or even any pretense at trying to determinine how many members of the community supported or opposed the proposed code of conduct, the SJW who proposed the code of conduct announced that the time for discussion was over, declared how pleased he was to see that "the vast majority of the Go community" supported the code of conduct, and informed the dissenters that their participation in the official Go forums was no longer required.

> *I hear and respect the dissenting opinions. In particular, I hear the concerns about limiting freedom of expression. Let me state this clearly: the official Go forums are not platforms for free speech. Your participation in them is a privilege, not a right. If you are not able to adhere to basic standards of respectful behavior then you are invited to leave.*

The shamelessness of the SJW's deceit is breathtaking, even when one knows perfectly well that SJWs always lie. In addition to lying about support from the vast majority of the community, most of whom did not express any opinion on the forums and may not have even heard about the code of conduct, the way in which the SJW blithely substituted this nebulous and as yet unspecified code of conduct for "basic standards of respectful behavior" is as remarkable as it is reprehensible.

Less than one month later, at the GopherCon 2015 conference, the SJW led a panel entitled the Code of Conduct & Diversity Discussion, which produced the following conclusions.

*Actionable suggestions made during the discussion:*

- *The code of conduct should be authored by multiple well-known people from the community.*

- *The conduct team should be 6–8 people, mostly from outside Google.*

- *The Go community should work with existing groups that represent minorities in tech.*

*Suggestions for GopherCon specifically:*

- *Provide women's T-shirts.*

- *Have a diverse range of people introduce the presenters.*

- *Pair up diversity scholarship recipients with established community members to help them meet people, etc.*

- *Provide a space at the conference operated by women to make them feel more welcome.*

And that is how just one SJW armed with a modicum of relative power is capable of not only enforcing the SJW Narrative throughout an entire community, but also taking control of that community and imposing thought-policing on it. The SJW in this case is merely an engineer who works for Google; his job gave him a certain status in the Go community, but his real power came from being the moderator of the official forum, which permitted him to launch the "discussion", control it, end it, and arbitrarily declare the outcome. Of course, Google is a very SJW-sympathetic institution, so this was also a case of an Amenable Authority; one doubts the SJW would have been able to so easily, and almost single-handedly, transform the pre-ordained forum conclusion into conference-approved action items expected to be binding on the entire community were it a large industry conference rather than a small one dominated by a single corporation.

Then again, the recent announcement of a new Advocacy Track at GDC intended to present "a number of topics that address new and existing issues within the realm of social advocacy" including topics ranging from "diversity to censorship to quality of life", may indicate that the SJWs are even more out of control in the technology field than anyone imagined.

In any event, lest you doubt the true purpose of the Go community's code of conduct, consider the responsible SJW's tweets in response to hearing a female programmer's claims to have been harassed. His furious white-knighting serves to graphically illustrate the SJWs' true priorities as well as their true faces when their concern masks happen to slip. I also quoted two responses by other SJWs to the SJW's chivalrous rant; note that "doxxing" was one of the original accusations that the SJWs used to justify calling #GamerGate a hate group.

> *This Industry Is Fucked. If you're one of the jerks who does this shit, please die in a fire. These assholes are holding us all back. So many amazing people crippled by this negativity and hate. So much wasted energy. If someone did that shit to me you can bet I would make a big fucking drama about it.*

*Sounds like a good opportunity for anonymous to start doxxing these people.*

*I really hope a Code of Conduct will help us deal with shit like this as a community.*

Notice that the Code of Conduct is expressly seen as a weapon intended to root out and destroy those the SJWs deem haters, as well as badthinkers, crimethinkers, and potential threats to the Narrative.

The third SJW objective is to keep out non-SJWs and anyone else who is considered likely to challenge either the Narrative or SJW control. This is why one often sees corporations engaging in seemingly unproductive actions such as turning away obviously more qualified candidates in favor of hiring less qualified people, promoting lazy and unreliable employees to management instead of the more valuable ones, and favoring mediocrity over excellence. It's also why a college degree and other credentials are now required for so many jobs where a high school diploma would have sufficed in the past.

After all, it's difficult to tell if someone who just graduated from high school is a reliable SJW or not. Aside from belonging to the gay-straight alliance, there isn't much to be learned from who was on the football team or the cheerleading squad. But when two applicants with college degrees are being compared, one of whom graduated from a state school with a degree in business and belonged to a fraternity versus a graduate of a liberal arts college with a degree in communications and memberships in a group dedicated to raising awareness and asking questions about common mixed-race and identity themes and cultural intersectionality, an LGBTQ support group for those who identify as queer, and the college's Women in STEM action committee, guess who the SJWs in HR are going to hire every single time?

SJW plots in the corporate world can be considerably more nefarious than the attempts to thought-police the Go community indicate. Consider what Eve T. Braun of Barclays, the large British financial institution, posted on the London Ruby User's Group mailing list explaining how she had successfully prevented the hiring of straight white men and other presumed non-SJWs.

*Two other things we implemented which aided the recruitment process:*

*We followed advice which is quickly becoming the industry norm. Never look at someones Github profile until you have made the decision to hire or not hire them and do not let it influence you. Github profiles tend to favor CIS White men over most minorities in a number of ways. CIS white men often have more spare time or chose to pursue building up an impressive portfolio of code rather than women or minorities who have to deal with things like raising children or institutionalised racism. Some in the SocJus community have even said that technically companies could possibly even be breaking discriminatory law by allowing peoples github profiles and publicly available code to influence their hiring decisions—watch this space.*

*We used Randi Harper's blockbot to assess applicants twitter profiles for problematic or toxic viewpoints. This may sound a bit extreme but some of the staff here suffer from Aspergers & PTSD and our top priority is to ensure that they don't get put in triggering situations. Making a wrong hire could present a scenario where the employee could be triggered on a daily basis by another employee with an oppressive viewpoint. Other than from a diversity standpoint, from a business standpoint these sorts of negative interactions can cost a company a huge amount of time & money in employees taking off*

> *sick days. When all the employees are on the same page the synergy*
> *in the office aids productivity.*

Notice in particular her claim that this behavior is "quickly becoming the industry norm". The worst part about this presumably recent development is the way it demonstrates that you may well have been the victim of SJW job-policing without even realizing it. What normal white man is ever going to apply for a job, fail to receive an interview request, and conclude on that basis that there is a conspiracy dedicated to keeping him from working at major corporations? Yet such SJW conspiracies observably exist.

As Margaret Thatcher noted, what appear to be harmless, but worthy objectives, such as Women in Tech initiatives and programs designed to help women and minorities get into STEM and game development, are actually stalking horses for much more dangerous SJW entryism. And once SJWs take control of an organization, or an industry, they are not easily dislodged.

# Chapter 7

# WHAT TO DO WHEN SJWS ATTACK

*What do SJW's want to achieve? Their goal is power and domination over the Western cultural narrative to manufacture a consensus that is aligned with their extreme far-left ideology. Since their ideas are so far removed from science, logic, and reason, this requires a complete control of information to disseminate their world view along with the complete silencing of those who contradict them.*

—"What Is A Social Justice Warrior?", RooshV, October 6, 2014

All of this is very well and good, but what exactly are you to do when SJWs attack you? The first thing to understand is that you will not be ready for it. SJWs always prefer to ambush an unsuspecting target who does not realize that he is vulnerable. As with the Spanish Inquisition (Monty Python edition), no one expects them. Even when the target is a veteran media figure, outspoken, controversial, and well-versed in the delicate dance between uncomfortable truth and unforgivable offense, he seldom sees the attack coming.

Consider, for example, the recent targeting of ESPN radio host Colin Cowherd, who was fired by ESPN for purportedly "making disparaging remarks about Dominicans". But not only were Cowherd's remarks not genuinely disparaging—he merely commented, truthfully, that despite the Dominican Republic not being known for having world class academics, professional baseball players from that country don't appear to have any problem grasping the complexities of baseball—he had made a number of considerably more controversial remarks in the past. And while ESPN may well have had other motives in firing Cowherd, as he was already leaving the network for Fox Sports, the fact remains that from the outside, it looked exactly like a textbook SJW ambush.

The cancelling of *Imus in the Morning* by CBS Radio in 2007 was much the same. Don Imus was a longtime radio shock jock, a four-time Marconi winner inducted into the National Radio Hall of Fame in 1989, and over the years he had said far more controversial things about everyone from Jews to blacks to Arabs to women, before he made the idle, unflattering, and frankly rather stupid comments about the Rutgers University women's basketball team that got him fired. Why were all the previous, more offensive comments overlooked while a few lame cracks about Rutgers basketball proved to be fatal to his career at CBS? Because those were the particular comments that Al Sharpton and other SJWs chose to weaponize in a successful attempt to target, discredit, and disemploy Imus.

Another reason these SJW ambushes are so often surprising is that as the repentant ex-SJW Ian Miles Cheong admitted in an interview with *Nerdland*, some of them have nothing to do with any animus for the target, but are launched in order for the SJW to obtain status within the social justice movement.

> *There were a lot of things I wished to say while I was a part of the social justice movement that I couldn't, because of "solidarity" and all sorts of other reasons. Dissent isn't tolerated in the movement*

*and stepping out of line will earn you whispers behind your back to ostracize you both socially and professionally. There's always a sense that your position in the movement is precarious and that unless you stand in front of the charge, you're going to be shut out and treated like a fairweather ally in spite of everything you've ever done to support the movement. It's for this reason that you see people falling over each other to see who can vilify their targets the most. At some point, the targets that get picked are guilty of nothing more than making a joke, or saying something that could potentially be interpreted as problematic, but isn't actually problematic.*

—"Games Media, Callout Culture and Gamers: an Interview With Ian Miles Cheong", John Sweeney, *Nerdland,* 27 July 2015

They're not just looking to be offended. They are hunting for opportunities to vilify people. These opportunistic attacks are impossible to anticipate because in many cases the target doesn't even know the SJW who complained to Human Resources or contacted the media, and even in the case of a public accusation on Twitter or a blog, he probably won't be aware of the attack until it has already blown up on social media because he doesn't follow his accuser. Sir Tim Hunt had probably made similar jokes about female scientists in laboratories before, but he had not made them in front of a status-seeking SJW like Connie St. Louis. Sensing an opportunity to make a name for herself by vilifying a Nobel Prize winner, she struck, and in doing so promptly put herself in front of the charge.

Now that you know an SJW attack will probably come as a surprise, you need to know what to do when it comes. And just as there are eight stages to an SJW attack, there are eight things you must keep in mind when responding to one.

# 1. Rely on the Three R's: RECOGNIZE it is happening. REMAIN calm. REALIZE no one cares.

The first thing to do when attacked by SJWs is to recognize that you are under SJW attack, remain calm, and realize that no one else cares. You need to understand that the attack is happening, accept that is happening, and refrain from the temptation to try to make it not be happening. Do not panic! Don't go running to others for help or sympathy, don't try to convince everyone around you how outrageous or unfair the accusation is, and don't explain to anyone how little you deserve the way you are being treated. They don't care. They really don't. Think about how little you cared when someone else was previously being attacked by SJWs and how little you did to support him, let alone take action to stop the attack. That's exactly how much your colleagues and acquaintances care about you being attacked and exactly how much they are going to do to stop it.

We are living in a time of fear and economic uncertainty. Everyone knows, on some level, that it could just as easily be them instead of you. Everyone is afraid of becoming a target. So while your colleagues might express sympathy to your face, more than a few of them are feeling at least a mild sense of relief that it is you, and not them, who are the current sacrifice laid out on the SJW altar. And some of them probably feel that even if you don't deserve to be portrayed as a sex criminal, a Klan member, or the bastard love child of Adolf Hitler and Chairman Mao, you kind of had it coming. After all, you really should have known better than to crack that joke, make that comment, forward that email, fire that hypersensitive minority, or ask out that marketing assistant, right?

The truth is that *it doesn't matter* why SJWs are attacking you. The only thing that matters is understanding that you are under attack *right now* and no one else is going to do anything about it. No one else is going to make it go away. To quote Mike Cernovich, the bestselling author of *Gorilla Mindset*,

"Life is easier once you realize nobody cares, except family and friends, *if you're lucky*".

In the case of my own targeting by the SJWs in SFWA, I was initially caught by surprise because my nominal offense was so trivial. Literally *scores* of other members, including three members of the SFWA Board, had done the same thing or worse, and moreover, the offense carried a specific penalty that had already been applied to me. It took me nearly a day to realize that they were seriously intending to take the inch I had given them and run a marathon with it, but once I understood that, it was very helpful to understand that they intended to expel me at any cost, by any means necessary, no matter what the relevant rules were.

## 2. Don't try to reason with them.

The second thing is to recognize that there is no way you are going to be able to reason your way out of the situation. Most people who come under SJW attack have the causality backwards. They think the attack is taking place due to whatever it is that they did or said. That's not the case. The attack is taking place because of who you are and what you represent to the SJWs: a threat to their Narrative. In most cases, the SJWs attempting to discredit and disemploy you already wanted you out long ago. They are simply using the nominal reason given as an excuse to get rid of you. And if the attack is more the result of SJW status-seeking rather than thought-policing, that's arguably even worse because if the motivation concerns them rather than you, there is absolutely nothing you can do about it.

The most important thing to accept here is the complete impossibility of compromise or even meaningful communication with your attackers. SJWs do not engage in rational debate because they are not rational, and they do not engage in honest discourse because they do not believe in objective truth. They do not compromise because the pure spirit of enlightened progressive social justice dare not sully itself with the evil of the outdated Endarkenment. They are the emotion-driven rhetoric-speakers of whom Aristotle wrote: "Before some audiences not even the possession of the exactest knowledge will make it easy for what we say to produce conviction. For argument based on knowledge implies instruction, and there are people whom one cannot instruct."

SJWs cannot be instructed. They have no interest whatsoever in talking to you or trying to understand you. Indeed, they will avoid you and do their best to minimize their communications with you while constantly talking about you and "explaining" the real meaning of your words and your nefarious true intentions to everyone else. They will also try to isolate you and cut you off from access to any relevant authority, to the media, and to neutral parties, the better to spin the Narrative without your interference. This is why it is vital that you do not agree to any confidentiality agreements or consent to keep your mouth shut while the SJW-driven "investigation" is proceeding.

## 3. Do not apologize.

The third thing to remember when undergoing an SJW-attack is to never apologize for anything you have done. I repeat: do not apologize. Do not say you are sorry if anyone's feelings were hurt, do not express regret, remorse, or contrition, and do not say anything that can be taken as an apology in any way. Just in case I am not being sufficiently clear, *do not apologize!*

Normal people seek apologies because they want to know that you feel bad about what you have done and that you will at least attempt to avoid doing it again in the future. They seek apologies within the context of an expectation of a better future relationship with you. This is why it is important to apologize to normal people you have harmed in some way; so that you can mutually repair the damaged relationship through the bonding process of repentance and forgiveness. When we sincerely apologize to those we have inadvertently offended, this process actually strengthens the relationship and often leads to improved mutual understanding.

None of that applies to SJWs. They don't care how you feel, they don't care about your future behavior, they don't expect to have a future relationship with you, and there is absolutely no chance they are going to forgive you for anything. You are, after all, a dangerous thought-criminal. When they push you for an apology after pointing and shrieking at you, what they are seeking is a confession to bolster their indictment. They are like the police down at the station with a suspect in the interrogation room, badgering him to confess to the crime. And like all too many police these days, the SJWs don't really care if you did it or not. They're just looking for a confession that they can take to the prosecutor.

This means that every apology, every compromise, and every attempt to find common ground will be viewed as a display of weakness, a lack of confidence, and damning evidence in the case concerning which they intend to prosecute you.

Therefore, the correct answer to a demand for an apology is always no. "Wouldn't it only make sense if..." No. "Can't we just..." No. "Wouldn't it be fair to..." No. "You have to admit..." No. "If you would just apologize..." No. "Don't you realize you hurt..." No.

Look at Hunt. Look at Eich. Look at everyone in your personal experience who has come under attack by SJWs. Did apologizing do them any good at all? Did apologizing reduce the intensity of the attacks on them, or did the SJWs keep attacking? An apology is not going to relieve the pressure on you; it is only going to increase it. To the SJW, an apology is merely the first step in the ritual act of abasement and submission, after which one must recant any previously expressed doubts about the Narrative and declare one's intentions of future adherence to it.

It is very educational to see what happens when one simply refuses to fall in line with their demands. A refusal to play along with their game quickly strips the mask of sanity from their faces and reveals the angry, shrieking madness underneath. Never forget that they have no certainty of a win without your compliance. So do not, under any circumstances, comply with any of their demands. Do not, under any circumstances, apologize, not even if you feel genuinely bad about what you have done or if you suspect you may have genuinely hurt someone's feelings.

Remember that they don't believe in forgiveness. They don't believe in repentance. All they are looking for is for you to condemn yourself so the show trial can begin. As one SJW has put it: "Apologies are not merely the end of a bad situation. They are the beginning of a promise to do (and be) better". So don't be under the false impression that an apology will put an end to anything. It will only serve as the start of the next stage of their attack.

Be aware that once they have launched an attack on you, they will press you hard for an apology and repeatedly imply that if you will just apologize, all will be forgiven. Do not be fooled! I have seen people fall for it time and time again, and the result is always the same. The SJWs are simply looking for a public confession that will confirm their accusations, give them PR cover, and provide them with the ammunition required to discredit and disemploy you. Apologizing will accomplish nothing more than hand them the very weapons they require to destroy you.

## 4. Accept your fate.

It is psychologically much easier to survive an SJW attack if you accept early on in the process that you are probably going to lose your job or be purged from your church, your social group, or your professional organization. Remember that if the SJWs were not confident they could take you out, they would not have launched their attack in the first place. They prey upon those they believe, rightly or wrongly, to be vulnerable. Even if you survive the attack, it's highly unlikely that your reputation will survive unscathed, as there are simply too many people who are inclined to split the difference in any conflict between two parties, no matter how crazy or dishonest they know one of the parties to be.

Be prepared to be disappointed by the behavior of some of the people you believe to be your friends. I have seen situations where people who have known the individual under attack for years—and even been good friends with them for decades—refuse to so much as put in a good word on behalf of the targeted individual for fear of being tarred with guilt by association. It can be deeply disappointing, even depressing, to see those you looked up to and admired fail when put to the test. But don't be angry with them or allow the anger you feel for the SJWs to be displaced onto those who have disappointed you. While they may have disappointed you with their cowardice, they are not your problem, they did not put you in the position you find yourself, and they are not your enemy.

Not everyone is cut out to be a fighter. Most people are conflict-avoidant to some degree, and many actually believe that being moderate and trying to see both sides of the story is a virtue. This is completely insane, of course, and hopelessly stupid when dealing with SJWs because SJWs always lie. Splitting the difference between the truth and a lie is not virtuous; it is providing effective cover for those who tell lies. Nevertheless, you will meet more than a few people who will attempt to square the circle or otherwise invent some fictitious middle ground that permits them to feel good about refusing to take sides. Throw in the tendency of many men to white-knight for even the most badly behaving woman, and you have to anticipate that the majority of people familiar with the situation are never going to give the accused party a fair shake when SJWs are attacking them.

You simply can't expect much in the way of truth in a world of liars. I have been blatantly lied about and libeled in the international media so many times that I don't even pay attention any longer. Even one of the lawyers who won a libel case for the *Guardian* was of the opinion that the newspaper had repeatedly libeled me, and that was before the SJWs in science fiction launched their hate campaign after the Sad Puppies near-sweep of the 2015 Hugo nominations and the *Guardian* began running what seemed like weekly articles about the terrible, no-good, very bad white male haters who hate women and minorities writing science fiction. So, don't worry about the lies. Don't waste your time trying to correct or counteract them. Just shoot them down when directly asked about them and otherwise ignore them. Ironically, the more they turn up the heat, the less you or anyone else will care about it.

It's like the Boy Who Cried Wolf; they can only call you racist, or sexist, or homophobic, or a bigoted shithole so many times before neutral observers who don't see anything out of the ordinary in your behavior begin to wonder if perhaps it isn't the accusing SJWs who have something wrong with them. The calmer you are, and the more you blow off their accusations with either a wry smile or open contempt, the faster those who are not involved will reach the correct conclusion.

On the practical side, don't hesitate, but immediately begin to make preparations in case the SJWs have correctly calculated your vulnerability to their attack. If your job is in jeopardy, start reaching out to your connections and see if it is possible to successfully jump ship before you are pushed. Talk to the corporate authorities to whom the SJWs are complaining and see if you can find a way to negotiate something that they can present to the SJWs as a win that will not do you any serious harm; remember that if the SJWs were truly in control, they would have simply whacked you without explanation or justification. Since the primary objective of the authorities is to sweep the whole thing under the rug, you may be able to get them to reassign you, transfer you, or even promote you so long as they can present it as a serious disciplinary action.

Only if you are either unusually valuable or have closer ties to the relevant authorities than the SJWs do should you attempt to turn the situation around on them. I have seen one situation where an SJW miscalculated, launched an attack, and was promptly fired for her efforts to put her personal politics ahead of the company's self-interest, but that is rare, and I have only seen it happen the one time. Remember that even though the authorities are seldom SJWs, they are usually sympathetic to them, and even when they are not, they are usually inclined to ensure that the squeakiest wheel always gets the grease. And no one is capable of outsqueaking an SJW.

This doesn't mean that you should despair or give up. Quite the contrary! It's only that you will be able to defend yourself much more effectively if you are not overly worried about the outcome. Ideally, you want to maintain the stoic state known as "Zero Fucks Given", or to put it in less vulgar terms, a state of total indifference as to the consequences. That's admittedly not always possible, but few things demoralize and discourage SJWs more than a target who is able to meet their most vicious attacks with little more than a wry smile before proceeding to punch them back twice as hard.

## 5. Document their every word and action

Most of the time, SJW purges are committed at least partially outside the organization's established rules and forms. You may not be an expert, but some of the people following along will be. Make sure every step in the process, and every piece of communication you receive from them, is documented, critiqued, and publicized. They will pull out all the stops to hide their actions in order to avoid public criticism, and in some of the more egregious cases, ridicule.

As noted in the previous chapter, the reason SJWs set up nebulous codes of conduct is that they want to be able to selectively impose discipline on those who question the Narrative in a manner they can interpret as "problematic" or "offensive" while avoiding the need to do so when one of their own breaks the rules. That's why they do their best to avoid clear lines of demarcation and detailed specifications of what is against the rules and what the punishment will be. They will even do their best to avoid committing anything to writing; it is not an accident that Sir Tim Hunt's wife received a telephone call from an individual at University College London who still remains publicly unidentified. Like insects scurrying about their business underneath a rock, SJWs prefer to operate in the dark and leave everyone else confused about what really happened.

By forcing them to show their hand in public, you allow others to see and understand what they are really up to. This may not be sufficient to save yourself from the ongoing attack, but it will almost certainly strengthen your negotiating position and will also help prevent the SJWs from blithely repeating the process against you or someone else in the future.

The first thing to do is force them to document their complaints and provide you with a copy of them. In a corporate setting, what will usually happen is that you will be verbally informed of a complaint by an accuser who is not identified. Instead of trying to defend yourself, admitting anything, or explaining your actions to the individual informing you, tell him that you will not discuss anything unless you receive a copy of the complaint in writing that is signed by both the accuser and the manager or executive who is informing you of the complaint. Then refuse to say anything further about the subject until it is provided. While the corporate executives react in confusion and disarray to your failure to go along with the execution program, obtain a copy of both the corporate rules and regulations as well as the state laws pertaining to employment and learn exactly what their options are. What will usually happen is that someone in human resources will invent some fictitious "policy" that prevents them from divulging the name of the SJW accusing you or the exact nature of your offense.

Again, force them to put it in writing or else simply ignore it. If they call you into their office or telephone you, inform them that you intend to record the conversation and ask for their permission to do so, or alternatively, show up in their office with a lawyer. (It doesn't even have to be a lawyer per se; it can simply be a friend wearing a suit who you introduce as your "representative".) They may back down at this point, especially if the nature of the attack is not based on something you yourself have written. Both the SJWs and the corporate authorities tend to be very leery of putting down anything on paper because they know that you are going to use it against them. But if they are dumb enough to provide you with documentation that relies on a policy that does not actually exist, that gives you a weapon you can take to a higher level as evidence of their bad faith and persecution.

At the same time, start documenting every violation by those you suspect to be SJWs or sympathetic to the campaign against you, past and present. This will help you demonstrate that the SJW campaign is personal and vindictive, and even if the authorities are SJWs themselves, it will help to undermine their position in the public eye. Also, be sure to save all of your emails and other information about everyone even tangentially related to the organization on a hard drive or memory stick that does not belong to the company. For example, once the attack on me began, I downloaded the entire SFWA Forum to my hard drive, and I now have an extensive record of science fiction SJWs who thought they were speaking privately among sympathetic parties saying dreadful things about everyone from the executives at Random House to self-published authors. It wasn't information I could use as a member of the Forum, due to the published Forum rules, but once I was kicked off it—and, as anticipated, I eventually was—I became free to make use of the information as I saw fit.

Remember that no one is going to believe anything you say. If it's not on paper, it doesn't exist. So, if there is even a remote chance it might be useful, document it. There is nothing SJWs fear more than a patient enemy who methodically documents their words and actions because they know that their lies will inevitably be exposed and used against them.

Don't forget the First Law. SJWs always lie! Don't take anything they say for granted, not even if it appears to be correctly sourced and cited. I cannot tell you how many times I have gone to verify something an SJW has confidently asserted to be true and discovered that he either lied, exaggerated, or completely mischaracterized the evidence upon which he was supposedly relying. Go through everything an SJW says with a fine-tooth comb, and document all the various "errors" and misrepresentations you will find. They will be there. I guarantee it.

Whatever you do, do not agree to any gag orders or sign any confidentiality agreements that will handicap your ability to use the documentation you have acquired to prevent them from spinning a Narrative about what happened. SJWs rely on secrecy, and once they know you have their actions documented, they will try very hard to tie your hands in a manner that will prevent you from making that information public.

## 6. Do not resign!

Do not resign! You must always keep in mind that their real goal is not to formally purge you but *to encourage you to quit* on your own. That allows them to publicly wash their hands of the affair and claim that your decision to leave was not their fault. They will often enlist more reasonable allies to approach you and tell you that it's not possible for you to continue any more, they will appeal to your desire to avoid conflict as well as to the good of the organization, and they will go on endlessly about the supreme importance of an amicable departure. Don't fall for it. Don't do their dirty work for them. Make them take the full responsibility for throwing you out, thereby ensuring they have to suffer the unpredictable long-term consequences of their actions.

No matter how deeply the deck is stacked against you, the outcome will always be in doubt unless you resign. You always have a chance to defeat them as long as you don't quit, and perhaps more importantly, refusing to quit buys you an amount of time that you can use to find another job before they manage to disemploy you. Considering how long you can reasonably expect to draw out the process, which will usually take not weeks, but months, you will considerably enhance your chances of finding alternative employment if you do not resign. While some people are under the impression that an inexplicable resignation will look better on their resume than being fired for cause, the fact is that it is much easier to find a job if you already have one. Not only that, but in many cases, the end result of the process is the choice between a forced resignation and an outright firing, so forcing the SJWs to go through the entire process is going to leave the average individual targeted by them materially better off than if he takes the bait and voluntarily retires when first pressured to do so.

There are no hard statistics available on this, but I would estimate that about one-half to two-thirds of the individuals who resign under pressure from SJWs would not have actually been forced to leave the corporation, institution, or organization if they had simply stood their ground, refused to apologize, and refused to resign. One of the main reasons they put so much pressure on people so early in their attack process is that they know they have a better chance of winning through psychological intimidation than they do through any legally valid process. The legal requirements of due process tend to stand directly in the way of the SJW desire for secrecy, their need to avoid documentation, and their preference for rapid purges that are completed before anyone else even realizes they are taking place.

That is why SJW-infested institutions often try to set up alternative pseudo-legal systems of the sort one sees at universities. These are systems that permit them to play prosecutor, judge, jury, and executioner while leaving neutral observers with the general impression that the accused has been given a fair trial. The growing number of codes of conduct being established by SJWs in various organizations are best understood as the larval stage of these faux-legal systems.

But regardless, the essential point remains: Do not resign! There is no advantage to you in doing so. As with apologizing, resigning is only going to make matters worse, not better, despite what the SJWs will promise you. They'll assure you that it will be best for everyone if you just quietly resign and go away, that it will be better for the organization to which your past contributions are greatly appreciated, and that the one last thing you can do for it now is to avoid making an uncomfortable scene. They'll promise that if you resign, you'll be able to quickly and quietly put the controversy behind you—and the moment you resign, they will alert the media, send out a statement to the entire organization, and begin waving your scalp like a bloody flag. The reason they need to publicize the news of your resignation is that one of their primary goals is to maintain the illusion of their irresistible power and inevitable victory. Therefore, despite their promises, they will always seek to advertise their victories in order to intimidate other potential crimethinkers into falling into line.

So don't believe them when they tell you that a resignation will make all the pain and humiliation go away, because SJWs always lie! And whatever you do, don't resign!

## 7. Make the rubble bounce.

Whether you survive the attempted purge or whether you don't, it's very important to observe who has defined himself as an ally, an enemy, or a neutral party during the process. The choices people make will pleasantly surprise you about as often as they disappoint you. Once everyone's choices have been made clear, your task is simple. Target the enemy at every opportunity. Hit them wherever they show themselves vulnerable. Play as dirty as your conscience will permit. Undermine them, sabotage them, and discredit them. Be ruthless and show them absolutely no mercy. This is not the time for Christian forgiveness because these are people who have not repented. These are people who are trying to destroy you and are quite willing to harm your family and your children in the process. Take them down and take them out without hesitation.

If you have any SJWs working under you, fire them. If you have an SJW relying upon you for something, play dumb and assure him that he'll get it on time. Then, fail to deliver, all the while continuing to offer reassurances that it's definitely going to be done next week. Above all, you must understand that the normal rules of live and let live are no longer in effect. The more you disrupt their activities and their daily routine, the more difficult they will find it to purge you. Assume that you are on your way out—if you've followed the previous advice given, you should already have your landing zone prepared and are only waiting for the right moment to exit—and salt the earth. Leave devastation in your wake so that it will take weeks or even months for them to try to recover from the damage of your purging.

I previously mentioned Voltaire's response to the aftermath of the Battle of Minorca. His famous quote, which is often misattributed to Napoleon, is appropriate here. *"Il est bon de tuer de temps en temps un amiral pour encourager les autres."* Which is to say, "it is wise to kill an admiral from time to time to encourage the others." Make the cost of purging you sufficiently painful that their amenable authorities will not be so amenable to SJW pressure in the future.

Of course, if you're in IT, you should probably check to see what the relevant laws are before you nuke the company's entire customer database or do anything too catastrophic. On the other hand, mistakenly deleting files that just happen to belong to the SJWs in Human Resources is an unfortunate accident that could happen to anyone, especially if you are able to make it look like malware or as if they did it themselves. Keep in mind that the object is to target your SJW enemies, not the entire organization, so it is best to keep the collateral damage to a minimum if you can.

Do you think that sounds too harsh? That's probably because you haven't had the experience of SJWs intentionally trying to end your career yet. It's remarkable of how your perception of what is fair and what is not will change once you've seen what the SJWs are willing to do.

Perhaps the best example of making the rubble bounce was what happened to Mozilla following Brendan Eich's resignation under pressure from the Mozilla board. Eich's supporters reacted to news of his being forced out with fury, and in addition to lodging a record amount of negative feedback with Mozilla, they began uninstalling Mozilla Firefox from their machines and replacing it with everything from Chrome to Pale Moon. Despite abject public pleas from a number of Mozilla contributors, 18 months after Eich's purge, Firefox usage remains significantly down.

> *To be clear, the browser's market share has been declining for five years. However, in reverse-engineering the figures listed above, one finds that the plunge in the past 12 months has been from 17.6 percent to the 11.6 percent Computerworld writer Greg Keizer cited (11.6 percent divided by 66 percent—1 minus 34 percent—is 17.6 percent). So in just one year, Firefox lost about 44 percent (6 points) of its five-year share loss of 13.5 points (25.1 percent minus 11.6 percent). In other words, the decline has seriously accelerated in the past year.*

> —"Is User Pushback Against Eich's Year-Ago Ouster Taking Down Mozilla?", *NewsBusters*, Tom Blumer, 8 March 2015

According to NetMarketShare, as of July 2014, Firefox usage is down to only 9.7 percent. And as further evidence of the effectiveness of the #UNINSTALLFIREFOX campaign, before the Eich purge, Mozilla Firefox represented 34 percent of the total pageviews at my blog, *Vox Popoli*. The percentage of

Firefox users there is currently down to 20 percent, which means that Mozilla has lost at least 5,017,260 pageviews from my readers alone.

That's a considerable amount of bouncing rubble!

And while Eich did not call for a Mozilla boycott and may not have had anything to do with it directly, his silence in response to the #UNINSTALL-FIREFOX campaign spoke volumes. Had he spoken out against it, his doing so would have taken a considerable amount of wind out of the campaign's sails. Instead, he simply stepped back and let events take their course at the expense of his enemies. Revenge is most effective when you don't even have to lift a finger to obtain it.

As you look for opportunities to make the rubble bounce, it is important that you also do your best to help out your allies whenever you can, even if they are the lukest of lukewarm friends. If you've got profitable accounts that you can hand over to those who have stood by you, hand them over before you go. (And if you've got problem accounts that are more trouble than they're worth, hand them over to your enemies.) Put in a good word with various managers and executives for your allies. Take them out to lunch and let them know that you've appreciated their support, particularly if they are people with whom you don't have much in common or with whom you don't get along. Often, your most useful and important allies will not be your friends, but people whose personalities and interests are very different from your own. Accept and embrace those differences; in a time of war, anyone shooting at your enemy is an ally who is more important than a friend.

With regards to neutrals, the main thing to keep in mind is that you're probably not going to be able to convince them of anything or talk them into taking a side. And that's all right. Accept their neutrality because if you put too much pressure on them to take the risk of trying to defend you, they will naturally gravitate towards the protective cover of the SJW camp, who have probably been putting pressure on them a lot longer than you have. Your primary objective should not be to win them over, but to prevent them from simply accepting the SJW's assertions at face value. To do so, keep your temper and calmly point out the observable pattern of inconsistencies, incoherencies, and lies. Always cast doubt about the SJW's opinion being credible concerning even the simplest and most straightforward of things. None of this will be sufficient to bring neutral parties over to your side, but it will make them much more reticent about accepting the SJW version of events. No one likes to get caught with his pants down and look like a credulous fool, after all.

So treat neutrals fairly, assume nothing of them either way, ask nothing of them, and refrain from judging them. Don't try to convince them to take a side. Never forget that it is better to be respected than loved by your allies, and it is better to be feared than respected by your enemies. Your enemies will never love you, so don't spare a moment's thought about trying to appease them or win them over.

## 8. Start nothing, finish everything.

This was a doctrine I learned in a martial arts dojo that was locally notorious for its brutality. The sensei drilled into us how important it was that we never throw the first punch, that we never act as the aggressor, and that we always resist any temptation to use our training as an excuse to throw our weight around. He taught us how to control our violent instincts and our reactions, to the point that all of us were able take a cheap shot or dangerous kick without losing our tempers or responding in anger. He did this through a simple, but very effective method; if you lost your temper at any time, but especially when sparring, you got to spend the next two-minute round fighting a black belt under orders to repeatedly knock you down.

I lost my temper once in my third year when a gold belt lashed out with a wild kick and nearly took out my knee. Furious, I doubled him over with a roundhouse kick, which was fine, but then put him down with a hook to the head when he was helpless, which was not. The sensei noticed this and said to one of the black belts, "Warren, why don't you explain to Mr. Day here why we control our tempers." Warren bowed, smiled, and promptly spent the next two minutes literally beating me down. I fought back as best I could, but ended up on my back five times, and on my belly once thanks to a particularly evil hook kick that caught me in the back of the head. I didn't require a second lesson in self-control; very few of us did.

In light of this history, it was interesting to see the Worldcon committee at Sasquan, which gave out the 2015 Hugo Awards, observe while in the course of a disciplinary proceeding concerning one of its attending members that "The puppies have a strong tendency to <u>retaliatory</u> action". This committee is nominally impartial, but their natural sympathies tend to lean pretty heavily towards the SJWs in science fiction. However, by resolutely refraining from attacking individuals who have not attacked us even though we know perfectly well they are not on our side, the Puppies have largely been able to avoid widening the conflict in science fiction beyond our war on the SJW cabal attempting to impose its diversity doctrine on the entire literary genre.

Another principle my sensei taught was, "Be slow to go, but when you go, you go 100 percent, and you don't stop until the opponent is incapacitated". This is a difficult lesson for most people to apply, especially in the context of an SJW attack, because there is a real sense of relief once the attack is over and the pressure is off. It is stressful to bear the brunt of daily personal attacks on social media, to be called names, and to be subject to death wishes and death threats, and this stress is compounded by the fact that it is usually felt by your friends and family as well. During the Sad Puppies 2 campaign of 2014, Larry Correia was subjected to such a vicious storm of lies by SJWs that family acquaintances were contacting his wife, concerned about her safety after reading assertions by SJWs who claimed that he was a wife beater.

Yes, that really happened. Even though you know the First Law of SJW, even though you are aware that they always lie, it's still hard to believe they would sink that low, isn't it? And yet, that's not even the nadir of their observed behavior!

Considering the level of stress you endure over the course of such an attack, it's completely understandable that the natural reaction is to want to put the whole thing behind you, regardless of the outcome. Whether they manage to purge you or whether they simply returned to the dark places where they lurk, it's finally over, and now you've got your life back again, right? Well, the bad news is that it is the rare SJW who is able to leave you alone after a run-in, especially if you managed to get in a few licks or publicly embarrass him in the process. The SJWs will keep taking shots at you, talking about you behind your back, and in general looking for a way to run you down or otherwise harm you if they can.

They do this because they are driven, in large part, by fear of being out-grouped, and the mere awareness of someone they perceive to be an enemy inside the in-group puts them under constant stress. One could write a book about it. Indeed, the Anonymous Conservative has. In *The Evolutionary Psychology Behind Politics*, he writes about how the SJW's have been observed to possess smaller amygdalas and less developed brain structures that are easily overwhelmed by "an intrusion of a reality they might not want to face, and cannot ignore".

In other words, even when the initial conflict is over, the SJWs are not going to leave you alone so long as they believe you to be a potentially vulnerable threat to them. This is why you have to be prepared to continue to up the ante until they finally reach the conclusion that they cannot possibly beat you and they are better off keeping their distance. Fortunately, SJWs are highly emotional, cowardly, and prone to depression, so demoralizing them tends to be considerably easier than you might imagine. They will still hate you, but after repeatedly meeting with staunch and confident opposition, they will usually decide to leave you alone and go in search of less difficult prey.

It may also be helpful to keep in mind that even in the age of social media, all press is still pretty much good press. For example, I was largely ignored by SJWs until I announced my candidacy for SFWA president. The month before that, November 2012, my total blog traffic was 745,857 Google pageviews. By the end of August 2013, during which the affair came to a head and the SFWA Board voted to expel me, my monthly traffic had risen to 1,308,334. It did drop down to an average of about a million per month as interest declined following the conclusion of the affair, but since then, it has steadily risen again to the point that my monthly traffic is now averaging 1,805,636 pageviews per month.

Clearly being vilified on a daily basis by SJWs around the world hasn't hurt me in the slightest. It's a little ironic, and more than a little amusing, that I now regularly see the volume of traffic that one of my leading SJW critics used to lie about having. And I tend to doubt that media outlets like *Newsweek* and the *Wall Street Journal* would be contacting me and requesting my opinion on various events were it not for SJW-run outlets like the *Guardian*, *Entertainment Weekly*, *National Public Radio*, *Popular Science*, *Wired* and *New Statesman* publicly attacking me.

Reward enemies who leave you alone by leaving them in peace. Reward enemies who insist on continuing hostilities with disincentivizing responses that are disproportionate to their provocations. And never forget, no matter what they do, they cannot touch your mind, they cannot touch your heart, and they cannot touch your soul.

# Chapter 8

# STRIKING BACK AT THE THOUGHT POLICE

*To the left, civil rights are like a subway: When you reach your stop, you get off. Meanwhile, I'll just repeat what I said yesterday: For the New Yorker's target audience, the equivalence of free speech advocates to "gun nuts" is a clear signal of where they're supposed to fall on the argument. But all I can say is that if the "speech nuts" do as well as the "gun nuts" have done over the past couple of decades, we'll be in pretty good shape. And the lesson from the "gun nuts" is: Don't compromise, don't admit that there's such a thing as a "reasonable restriction," don't back down, and keep pointing out that your opponents are liars and hypocrites. And punish the hell out of politicians who vote with the other side.*

—Glenn Reynolds, *Instapundit*, 11 August 2015

The reason SJWs have been so successful since the 1990s is that for more than two decades, they simply did not meet with any serious or organized resistance. #GAMERGATE represented the first serious organized resistance to them, and in only one year, the intrepid warriors of the gamer community have inspired similar resistance movements to surface in science fiction, in comics, and in romance. Echoes of #GAMERGATE have begun to appear in the popular culture, as Donald Trump not only refused to kowtow before Fox News's Megyn Kelly flashing of the SJWs' Woman card during the U.S. presidential debate but afterwards declared political correctness to be a big problem in the U.S.A. Trump's unexpected popularity in the polls is, to a large extent, a consequence of his willingness to confront the SJW Narrative and speak the truth as he sees it.

#GAMERGATE tactics are also beginning to be adopted by other groups for unrelated purposes, as there is a distinctly GG tone to the anti-Planned Parenthood memes that have been cropping up on Twitter ever since The Center for Medical Progress began releasing its sting-videos that showed Planned Parenthood employees openly discussing the sale of human organs taken from the infants it aborts. American immigration opponents have also successfully tarred some of the leading Republican candidates as well as their media supporters with the #CUCKSERVATIVE hashtag, much to the dismay of both the G.O.P. elite and the *New York Times* alike. It is therefore little wonder that SJWs are terrified of #GAMERGATE and see it as their most fearsome enemy. Increasingly paranoid SJWs are beginning to see #GAMERGATE lurking under their beds, and it should come as no surprise that #GAMERGATE would, in its wry and ruthless manner, mercilessly mock their fears.

- *I'm now starting to see #GAMERGATE show up in completely unrelated places as an all purpose boogieman for every SJW gripe imaginable.* —Literally Jamie

- *That time they took American currency off the gold standard? Totally #GAMERGATE* —Mingo

- *Remember that meteor that made the dinosaurs extinct? That was #GAMERGATE* —Reptilian Hunter

- *That time you lost your car keys… Guess what, we did it. Muhahahahah* #GAMERGATE —Mr. Airconditioning

- #GAMERGATE *cancelled Firefly* —ASaltMineNamedZilla

Damn you, #GAMERGATE! Is there no evil to which you will not stoop?

But the success of GamerGate notwithstanding, to date the anti-SJW campaign has been predominantly reactive in nature. And while it is certainly encouraging to see battles being won against SJWs in various industries, to see SJW advances turned back, and to see the anti-SJW resistance grow and spread, one cannot win a cultural war while remaining on the defensive and always conceding the initative to the enemy. That is why it is important to step back from the ongoing battles and to consider the anti-SJW war from a more strategic perspective.

# Strategic Principle #1: Know the SJW and Know Yourself

It is perhaps helpful to remember that war is a form of politics. Or, to put it as one of the great strategists of history, Carl von Clausewitz, phrased it, "War is merely the continuation of politics by other means". This is not a metaphor, for as Clausewitz also wrote, "War therefore is an act of violence to compel our opponent to fulfill our will". Cultural war of the sort in which the SJWs are engaged is an act of social pressure to compel their opponents to fulfill their will. So, while the means are different, the same strategies, and in some cases, even the same tactics, will apply to both war and cultural war alike.

This observation is not unique to me. The influential military strategist, William S. Lind, is well-known in military circles around the world for his development of the concept of 4th Generation War. Being his editor and publisher, I have the distinct honor and privilege of speaking with him on a regular basis, and it was intriguing to hear him observe, after reading about #GAMERGATE in his local newspaper, that it was an obvious application of 4GW principles to the cultural war. The #GAMERGATE philosophy of decentralization, independent action, open enrollment, and media-focused activity is an effective recreation of highly effective insurgencies that are well known to every military historian.

And since there is a direct connection between military strategy and cultural war strategy, that means a strategy to strike back at the SJWs should begin in the same place that effective military strategy begins, which is to say Sun Tzu. While most of his advice concerning spies and troop movements is not applicable to cultural war, there is one foundational concept that is as applicable to the anti-SJW resistance today as it was to the battles of the Warring States period in ancient China.

> *If you know the enemy and know yourself, you need not fear the result of a hundred battles. If you know yourself but not the enemy, for every victory gained you will also suffer a defeat. If you know neither the enemy nor yourself, you will succumb in every battle.*
>
> *—The Art of War*, Sun Tzu

Sun Tzu's maxim illustrates the key advantage that every anti-SJW possesses over his SJW enemies. Remember: SJWs always lie! And the first person to whom they lie is always themselves. The SJW doesn't know himself because he can't bear to admit the truth to himself; it is his denial of objective reality that is the foundation of his SJWism. Nor does the SJW know his opponent, because making the effort to understand exactly who and what his opponent is will almost always contradict the SJW Narrative.

For example, SJWs have regularly called me a white supremacist, a fascist, a neo-Nazi, and a Nazi because it suited their rhetorical needs, not because they knew anything about me. Once I made the fact that I am an American Indian known, many of them had the sense to quickly drop the "white supremacist" claims, but some, like Jeet Heer of *The New Republic*, have not, simply because they did not want to admit that I had the ability to play the Red card against them. In like manner, the SJWs in science fiction have tried to claim that despite being married to a black woman, Sad Puppies 3 leader Brad Torgersen is a racist.

Even when an SJW knows the truth about his enemy, he cannot admit it, accept it, or take it into account so long as it contradicts the current Narrative. As per Sun Tzu's advice, this means that the anti-SJW will always have a powerful advantage as long as he is honest about himself and honest about them. And in truth, this lack of knowledge about themselves and others is one reason why the SJWs are so readily defeated by their opponents whenever those opponents bother to actually show up and fight.

The way this tends to work out in a practical sense is that SJWs are all attack and no defense. If you can survive the attack and counterattack, you will often be surprised to learn how easy it is to send them reeling in disarray.

## Strategic Principle #2: Secure Your Base

The second step in striking back is SJW-proofing your organization. The core SJW strategy is to invade and take over any institution or organization that can advance their cause but to retain their attachment to the cause rather than to the institution. That is why they will not hesitate to destroy it rather than see it used for any purposes besides their own. Due to their entryist tactics, most institutions never realize they have been invaded until it is too late and their institutional high ground has already been taken over. At the universities, it is the administration. In corporations, it is the Personnel and Human Resources departments. In local government, it is the school boards and the employment unions. In open-source software, it is the community management positions.

Jerry Pournelle was one of the first to recognize the way SJW entryism functions in his Iron Law of Bureaucracy, which states:

> *In any bureaucratic organization there will be two kinds of people: those who work to further the actual goals of the organization, and those who work for the organization itself. In all cases, the second type of person will always gain control of the organization, and will always write the rules under which the organization functions.*

In every case, the first SJW's primary objective is to bring more SJWs inside the organization. To give one example, consider the role-playing game publisher Modiphius, which is in the process of producing a new Conan RPG called *Robert E. Howard's CONAN Adventures In An Age Undreamed Of.* In addition to twenty highly experienced men, they hired a woman by the name of Monica Valentinelli, who has solid credentials in the RPG field, having been the lead developer and writer for the *Firefly* RPG. And yet, what was Valentinelli's first order of business? To fire off this tweet.

> *I am looking for female freelance writers to work on the Conan RPG. If you are interested, hit me up at monica AT mlvwrites DOT com.*

Never mind that the writing team already consisted of "long time TSR stalwart Thomas M Reid (*Dragon Mountain, Tales of the Comet, Forgotten Realms, Planescape, Ravenloft, Temple of Elemental Evil* novel), Kevin Ross (*Masks of Nyarlathotep, Cthulhu by Gaslight, Colonial Lovecraft Country, Down Darker Trails*), Lou Agresta (*Snows Of An Early Winter, Slave Pits of Absalom, Freebooters Guide to the Razor Coast*) and Scott Oden (Best-selling author of the historical fiction novels *Men of Bronze, Memnon,* and *The Lion of Cairo*), Valentinelli's priority was to find "female freelance writers". After all, what would *Robert E. Howard's CONAN Adventures* be without the female touch?

For the SJW, the cause is always more important than the task at hand or his employer's interests.

SJWs don't see anything wrong with this behavior. Consider one science fiction SJW, who blithely announced on File 770, "One of our librarians is a NESFA member, which I think is at least partially responsible for us having a particularly good SF selection (including many NESFA Press books)". Imagine that. A librarian who belongs to a certain group making sure that his library purchases many books that just happened to be published by that group. Yet if you asked him about his actions, he would swear up and down that he is only making his selections on the basis of merit, not personal bias. This behavior is absolutely standard practice for SJWs.

Just as J.S. Mill advocated long ago, many institutions, from the Anglican Church to the Boy Scouts of America, have fallen to SJW entryism. That is why it is absolutely vital to not only build structural defenses against their invasions, but also to periodically sweep your organization to make sure that it remains SJW-free. It may seem a little ironic to have to police your organization yourself in order to prevent it from being thought-policed, but the sad historical fact is that you have to choose between one and the other. Some practical ideas for SJW-proofing your organization will be addressed in the next chapter.

## Strategic Principle #3: Focus primarily on morale.

Two of the authors I have the privilege to publish, Martin van Creveld and William S. Lind, have spent decades studying the art and history of war. Both Van Creveld, a military historian, and Lind, a political and military strategist, very heavily stress the signal importance of morale, particularly when it comes to long-term conflict. Lind follows Col. John Boyd's lead in considering the moral level of war (which is the primary factor that determines the morale of the soldiers) to be the highest and most significant level of war, more important than the mental and physical levels on which strategy, operations, and tactics are usually discussed.

Nor are Boyd and Lind alone in this. In his highly influential book, *The Transformation of War*, Van Creveld, who is Israel's leading military historian, considers practically every counterinsurgency around the world from the ancient Maccabees to the Second Palestinian Intifada before concluding that nothing, not even repeated victories on the battlefield, is as important as maintaining a high level of morale and discipline throughout the fighting forces. And he draws particularly on the experience of the British in Ireland to conclude that this is every bit as important for the stronger side as for the weaker one.

> *A small, weak force confronting a large, strong one will need very high fighting spirit to make up for its deficiencies in other fields. Still, since survival itself counts as no mean feat, that fighting spirit will feed on every victory, however minor. Conversely, a strong force fighting a weak one for any length of time is almost certain to suffer from a drop in morale, the reason being that nothing is more futile than a string of victories endlessly repeated.*

—Martin van Creveld, *The Transformation of War*, 1991

Do these military principles translate to the cultural war? Absolutely. One of the most noteworthy things about participating in #GAMERGATE was the very high level of importance that was placed on maintaining the morale of the GamerGaters participating in the various ops. Despite the massive imbalance of power, with literally the entire gaming and mainstream medias attacking an extraordinarily ragtag group of gaming freaks who span the political spectrum and had virtually nothing in common with each other except their support for ethics in game journalism, the constant barrage of positive memes being produced by #GAMERGATE artists and spread over social media, combined with the daily messages of encouragement from other GamerGaters, kept people's spirits up.

Some, like Daddy Warpig in particular, were tireless, tweeting dozens of times a day. Others whose enthusiasm flagged were not criticized, but were encouraged to take a break for a month or two, after which they came back refreshed, motivated, and ready to send emails. Images that mimicked old World War II recruitment posters were created, and the #GamerGate mascot Vivian James appeared everywhere from Kukuruyo's excellent *Gamer-Gate Life* cartoon to the meetups that took place everywhere from Texas to Tel Aviv.

#GamerGate also directly targeted the morale of its enemies. In addition to subjecting the journalists and their advertisers to an unending deluge of email, we took over enemy hashtags, produced memes that mocked and parodied their memes, and so effectively drove them from social media that anti-GamerGater Randi Harper resorted to creating a blockbot that would permit anti-GamerGaters to mass-block tens of thousands of #GamerGate accounts on Twitter, including mine, in order to shield their delicate psyches from #GamerGate's non-stop intellectual artillery.

> *@voxday is on the ggAutoblocker's blocklist.*
>
> *@voxday is on The Block Bot's blocklist (Level 2).*

You should be aware that you have a very important strategic advantage vis-a-vis the SJWs with regards to morale. A large percentage of SJWs are prone to various forms of mental illness; being competitive with regards to their victimhood, it is not at all uncommon for them to openly brag about being on various antidepressants and other psychiatric medications. I have been told by observers that the *majority* of commenters on several SJW sites have publicly made reference to their being prescribed such medications. Because so many of them are miserable and depressed, the strategy of repeatedly hammering SJW morale with dark messages of inevitable failure, doom, and defeat tends to be considerably more effective than it is when aimed at normal, happy, self-confident individuals.

Remember that morale is more important than objectives, more important than leaders, more important than organization, and is even more important than victories. In World War II, the German Wehrmacht made highly effective use of rapidly counterattacking after losing a position, a policy known as the Doctrine of the Stabilized Front. Their objective was to destroy the advancing enemy before he could consolidate his gains. Moreover, as Van Creveld noted, there are few things that demoralize a successful enemy more than the evidence that his hard-won victory has accomplished nothing. Although it may sound counterintuitive, there are few things that demoralize an organization more than meeting with futile success after futile success.

As long as your morale remains high, you cannot lose, and the SJWs cannot win. Consider, for example, how the SJWs are already visibly demoralized. They genuinely thought they'd won the cultural war once and for all, only to discover that the long bitter war has barely even begun.

> I'm so WEARY of these assholes. This is supposed to be FUN. It isn't supposed to be a long, bitter war. I hope the Puppies are fucking trounced in disgrace at the Hugo's. I hope "no award" wins for most of the categories they flooded. As wonderful as that will be it will just make them more bloodthirsty, bigoted and pigheaded. This drama won't end with the Hugo's. I am so fucking tired of my favorite things being overshadowed by the looming, gross specter of these fragile idiots. Gaming, science fiction and fantasy have always involved women, POC and the LGBTQ community. The fact that this is suddenly a shocking newsflash terrible enough for them to take up metaphorical arms against us in 2015 is cause for despair.
>
> —Eldritch, io9

He's absolutely right to despair because we have not only taken up metaphorical arms, we are methodically forcing them into one retreat after another.

The media influence on which they rely so heavily has turned out to be worse than useless; it is our primary source of new recruits. Just as #GamerGate has gone from strength to strength in the face of intense media opposition, the number of both Rabid Puppies and Vile Faceless Minions have increased as a direct result of the repeated media hit pieces.

## Strategic Principle #4: Research, dig, and document.

Remember the First Law: SJWs always lie! That means there is, without question, the gold of truth hidden somewhere in the hills of whatever Narrative the SJWs are attempting to defend. It's there; you only have to find it. The Third Law can be of use here because if an SJW is accusing you of something dishonest, there is a very good chance that he is engaging in that very activity himself.

As I mentioned before with regards to documentation, take nothing at face value. Check to see that every i is dotted, every t is crossed, and every number is correct. One thing I've noticed is that SJWs tend to be somewhat innumerate, so they frequently fail to realize how absurd their assertions are whenever numbers are involved. Another favored tactic of the SJW is the definitional switcheroo, so always be careful to check precisely how they are defining words since you can often catch them substituting bizarre definitions of their own concoction in order to slip things past an insufficiently careful reader. SJWs absolutely hate dictionary definitions because having an objective limit on their ability to claim X is really Y significantly reduces their opportunity to play word games.

Also, SJWs are lazy. They're not used to being questioned, and they rely heavily upon whatever their fellow SJWs tell them, so it's usually pretty easy to catch them out in basic errors of fact as well as logic. Even when their errors are trivial or irrelevant, you can use those mistakes to cast doubt upon their reliability and undermine their credibility.

Operation Dig Dig Dig is not one of the better-known #GAMERGATE ops, but the fact that any GamerGater could rapidly draw upon a wide selection of contacts, references, citations, draft emails and the results of research by other GamerGaters from the various repositories set up around the Internet was a major factor in #GAMERGATE's success. DeepFreeze, a journalism reference source, with seven different sections devoted to Censorship, Dishonesty, Intimidation, Collusion, Corruption, Cronyism, Sensationalism, and Trivia, is one that I have found particularly useful.

## Strategic Principle #5: Build strategic alliances

You are not unique. You are not alone. You are not the first person to be targeted by SJWs and you will not be the last. The problem is that so few people possess a) the courage to withstand repeated SJW attacks, b) the ability to take the offensive, and c) the willingness to help others who are being attacked. After surviving an attack, most people feel drained and have absolutely no desire to go through the experience again. It can be stressful, particularly if you are a conflict-avoidant person, and it is often unpleasant to have your name besmirched, your character befouled, your motivations questioned, your intentions declared to be false, and your friends and family declared to be evil collaborators.

This means that you should not reach out to everyone who is inclined to be sympathetic or anti-SJW, but only to those on whom you can rely to be staunch under fire and willing to show up when you call. This is much more important than mere friendship or general agreement about life, the universe, and everything because the SJWs will inevitably attempt to apply the Alinsky tactic of isolating you. Ironically, at the very time the SJWs in science fiction were attempting to separate Larry Correia and Brad Torgersen from me, other SJWs were attempting to separate me from someone they fear and hate even more, the neomasculinist Bane of Canada, RooshV.

They were unsuccessful in both cases; the two Sad Puppies leaders resolutely refused to either disassociate from me or disavow me (while quite rightly refusing to accept any responsibility for my actions), while I promptly, and publicly, swore blood brotherhood with Roosh despite the fact that he is a hedonistic pagan playboy and I am an evangelical Christian with hermitic inclinations. We may not agree on many things, but I'd rather have Roosh, an experience-hardened veteran of many a public relations battle, at my back than a company of evangelical Christians who will burst into tears and flee as soon as the first barrage of "racist sexist homophobia" begins to land.

It's one thing to reach out. To cement a strong strategic alliance that will be effective over time, you have to be a good ally yourself. Be quick to come running when your allies call. Retweet their tweets. If you're on Facebook, like their posts. If you've got a blog, provide an excerpt to their posts along with a link to help build their traffic. Pay closer attention to them than usual if you know they're under attack and provide them with tactical advice if you've got any and moral support if you don't. If you're in the media, look for an excuse to talk about your allies and build them up wherever possible. If you know of a job opening or some other opportunity, see if any of your allies are a fit for it before you advertise it to the public.

Or, you know, write a foreword to their book for them....

The Left has historically done an excellent job of this, so much so that their strategic alliances often looked more incestuous than strategic. The Four Horsemen of the New Atheism, Richard Dawkins, Daniel Dennett, Sam Harris, and the late Christopher Hitchens were one particularly effective such alliance; as I noted in *The Irrational Atheist*, "here Dawkins is lionizing Harris's 'wonderful little book', there he is favorably quoting Dennett favorably quoting himself, while the works of Dawkins and Dennett top Harris's list of recommended reading."

To beat the Left, you have to be reliably better than the Left. That means forging stronger alliances and always looking out for the interests of your allies as assiduously as you look out for your own.

## Strategic Principle #6: Select your targets and stick to them.

Perhaps because they are so sensitive to social status, SJWs are extraordinarily hierarchical. They tend to form little rabbit warrens around higher-status SJWs and psychologically identify with them. These "chief rabbits" tend to make ideal targets for several reasons. First, they are always terrified of losing their status and have little choice but to respond to direct attacks lest they look cowardly and risk losing the support of their followers. Second, they tend to be extreme SJWs, and their lies and misrepresentations tend to be more outrageous and more easily exploited than those of the average SJW. Third, because they have public platforms, exposing them and taking them down has a natural tendency to elevate the critic's profile. Fourth, taking down a "chief rabbit" SJW tends to have the knock-on effect of demoralizing the lesser SJWs who look up to him.

The Three Laws of SJW can be very useful in identifying a target. Because SJWs always project, focus on the areas they tend to complain about or criticize most. Those who go on about sexual harassment are probably prone to creeping and stalking. Those who bang on about homophobia likely have some orientational issues. And those who make a particular point to strike a pose about anti-Semitism are the most likely to have a Nazi armband somewhere in a drawer.

Institutions seldom make good targets because the individuals who run them are so easily replaced. Even when it is necessary to target an institution for practical reasons, it is always more effective to target specific individuals within the institution rather than the institution itself.

Once you've identified your target, stay focused on it. You'll know your shots are striking home if other SJWs rush to the targeted SJW's defense, but don't permit yourself to be distracted and drawn off to engage with these secondary targets. Ignore them for the time being and stay focused on the original target. Be patient. You can always get around to them later.

## Strategic Principle #7: Keep the moderates in check.

Moderates are the people who are nominally on your side but don't have the courage to take on the enemy directly and never hesitate to offer advice and criticism to those who do. They generally mean well, but they have a tendency to believe that goodwill, hand-holding, and being open-minded will inspire even the most lunatic, hate-filled SJW to see sweet reason. Even worse, this belief often causes them to attack their putative allies in order to prevent their allies from attacking the enemy since attacking the enemy would get in the way of the rapprochement that the moderate is certain will happen with the very next concession.

Moderates are usually nice people who want to think well of everyone, and they make for very good ambassadors and diplomats. Unfortunately, they usually prefer appeasement to offense, and they are far more inclined to shoot at their own side than they are at the enemy. One of the readers at *Vox Popoli*, Civis Silas, described their unreliable tendencies in an amusing little dialogue describing a fictional duel of honor being refereed by a moderate.

> Moderate: Okay, gentlemen, or rather, gentle cisgendered humans, you will take five paces, then turn and shoot. SJW has won the coin toss and he will shoot first. Understood?
>
> SJW: Xir.
>
> Moderate: What?
>
> SJW: Xir is my pronoun of choice. Also, I identify as Otherkin. Specifically, a llama.

Moderate: Right. I do apologize, I certainly didn't mean to offend you. Xir will shoot first.

Anti-SJW: Wait, how did he win the coin toss? He called heads AND tails!

Moderate: Xir!

SJW: *smirks*

Anti-SJW: Fine, whatever. It's not like he could hit the broad side of a football stadium.

Moderate: Xir!

Anti-SJW: Seriously?

Moderate: It's only polite. Very well. Are you both ready?

Anti-SJW: Sure.

SJW: Time to meet social justice, hatelord!

Moderate: One...

SJW: *immediately turns and aims pistol at Anti-SJW's back.*

Moderate: *looks at SJW disapprovingly.* Two...

SJW: CHECK YOUR PRIVILEGE! *Fires and completely misses.*

Anti-SJW: What the hell? *turns around.* You bastard!

SJW: How dare you turn around! That's against the rules! Hey, he's turning around!

Moderate: Anti! You must take three more paces before you may turn around and return fire!

Anti-SJW: *incredulous.* He shot at me after two!

SJW: Xir!

Moderate: Do not lower yourself to xir's level! Winning the wrong way is worse than losing!

Anti-SJW: Are you out of your freaking mind? *aims at SJW*

SJW: *cowers in fear and wets himself. Sorry, xirself.*

Moderate: How dare you! *draws pistol and aims it at Anti-SJW.* If you do not turn around this very instant, I shall shoot you myself, you dishonorable cur!

How can you identify a moderate? He is the man who only shoots at his own side and never at the enemy. Moderates merit friendly civility, but no respect. They are often useful, if irritating allies, but do not permit them any input into strategy and tactics or decision-making. And do not accept them as leaders except of their own moderate faction. They are considerably worse than useless in that regard because they are constantly trying to find a middle ground that quite often does not exist.

This isn't to say that moderates can't learn. I have known a few who have done so, gradually and over time, mostly by virtue of having their "friends" on the other side repay their steadfast good will with repeated betrayals and regular stabs in the back. But they still need to be regarded with an amount of suspicion and kept out of any leadership position.

## Strategic Principle #8: Be antifragile.

I cannot too highly recommend Nassim Nicholas Taleb's 2012 book, *Antifragile: Things That Gain from Disorder*, or too strongly stress the importance of applying the principles he explains in it to your life, especially if you are going to take a stand against the SJW Narrative. It should be your goal to become "a thing that gains from disorder" because disorder is the natural state of the world, particularly now that SJWs have become increasingly influential within it. Antifragility in this context means you have a maximal degree of flexibility, a high level of freedom of movement, sufficient psychological strength to withstand collective social pressure, and a lack of vulnerability to the usual SJW tactics of disqualification, discrediting, and disemployment.

For example, James Watson was not antifragile despite his sky-high scientific status because, even as Chancellor Emeritus, he did not have effective control over the Cold Spring Harbor Laboratory, which fired him after he challenged the SJW Narrative on race. Sir Tim Hunt was not antifragile for multiple reasons, but the particular fragility that proved fatal was that his wife was susceptible to manipulation by the unknown administrator at University College London who lied to her and told her that her husband could resign quietly. (In fairness to Hunt's wife, absolutely nothing about Sir Tim's subsequent behavior indicates that he would have been strong enough to withstand the social pressure that resulted from Connie St. Louis's ambush on his own.)

SJWs will always seek out your weak points and direct the greater part of their efforts there. Recall how in response to the Sad Puppies 2 campaign, the science fiction SJWs went after Larry Correia's wife because they knew the International Lord of Hate could not have cared less what they thought of him personally. It can be very useful, therefore, to make a habit of regularly feeding them false information in order to encourage them to focus their vicious energies on nonexistent weaknesses. And it is even more useful to not have any weaknesses for them to exploit.

Targeting employment is one of their standard routines, which is why it was so amusing when Daniel Vavra, a pro-GamerGate developer and the designer of *Mafia*, told an SJW that he had received the complaint about him that she sent to Warhorse Studios, which he co-founded; that is a beautiful example of antifragile employment.

No one is entirely bulletproof, but it is very helpful to not be fragile when the SJWs come after you.

In summary, the thought police can be beaten, though seldom without risk and never without effort. But even the most fragile and vulnerable man can resist them because your thoughts are always free.

*Und sperrt man mich ein im finsteren Kerker,*
*das alles sind rein vergebliche Werke.*
*Denn meine Gedanken zerreißen die Schranken*
*und Mauern entzwei: Die Gedanken sind frei!*

And if I am thrown into the darkest dungeon,
All these are futile works,
Because my thoughts tear all gates
And walls apart: The thoughts are free!

# Chapter 9

# WINNING THE SOCIAL JUSTICE WAR IN THE WEST

*I believe that 'social justice' will ultimately be recognized as a will-o'-the-wisp which has lured men to abandon many of the values which in the past have inspired the development of civilization-an attempt to satisfy a craving inherited from the traditions of the small group but which is meaningless in the Great Society of free men. Unfortunately, this vague desire which has become one of the strongest bonds spurring people of good will to action, not only is bound to be disappointed. This would be sad enough. But, like most attempts to pursue an unattainable goal, the striving for it will also produce highly undesirable consequences, and in particular lead to the destruction of the indispensable environment in which the traditional moral values alone can flourish, namely personal freedom.*

—F.A. Hayek, *Law, Legislation and Liberty, Volume 2: The Mirage of Social Justice*, 1976

It may seem difficult to imagine a time when social justice has been swept from the scene and SJWs are as irrelevant as Whigs, Girondists, or Mensheviks, but every ideology fades in time, and those founded on falsehoods tend to fade faster than most. The fact that most SJWs would genuinely deny that they are socialists or that they seek to destroy Western civilization means that sooner or later, they will be forced to confront the fact that the goals they seek, Equality, Diversity, and Inclusiveness, are utterly incompatible with personal freedom, societal wealth, and advanced technological civilization.

There are very few SJWs who would be willing to give up indoor plumbing or their iPhones for their ideals. The fact that they cannot see the contradiction now does not mean they will always be unable to do so, particularly given the way in which their corrupted institutions are falling into rapid decline, one after the other, and being replaced by radical new institutions. The public schools can no longer educate, so people are turning to homeschooling. The universities can no longer provide liberal arts educations, so people are becoming technology-assisted autodidacts. The banks no longer loan, the state and local governments no longer provide basic public services, the military does not defend the borders, the newspapers no longer provide news, the television networks no longer entertain, and the corporations are increasingly unable to provide employment.

Even as the institutions have been invaded and coopted in the interests of social justice, they have been rendered unable to fulfill their primary functions. This is the great internal contradiction that the SJWs will never be able to positively resolve, just as the Soviet communists were never able to resolve the contradiction of socialist calculation that brought down their economy and their empire 69 years after Ludwig von Mises first pointed it out. One might call it the Impossibility of Social Justice Convergence; no man can serve two masters, and no institution can effectively serve two different functions. The more an institution converges towards the highest abstract standard of social and distributive justice, the less it is able to perform its primary function.

It is possible—indeed, it is likely—that the SJWs will not recognize the utter impossibility of the task they have made a societal imperative any more quickly than the Soviets grasped the futility of socialist calculation. On the other hand, the SJWs are in considerably less control in the West than the Communists were in the Soviet Union and Western society is already approaching a serious crisis, if not a complete collapse of its systemic infrastructure.

As a sane member of the citizenry who values the various benefits of Western civilization, it falls to you to try to turn back the tide of SJW insanity before everyone learns about the impossibility of social justice convergence the hard way. While it might be satisfying to imagine the face of the SJW of your acquaintance when he learns what his ideal society actually looks like, the fact that you would have to live in that post-apocalyptic environment too should be enough to motivate you to deny yourself the potential pleasure.

It would be much better to defeat the SJWs, roll back their gains, negate their influence in the culture, and destroy their poisonous and destructive ideology. The following is a seven-point strategy for going about accomplishing that, based on a basic tactical principle. Once the enemy sets a precedent by utilizing a certain tactic, you are not only free to utilize that tactic against him, but *you must do so* if you wish to prevent him from continuing to use it successfully against you.

This is a principle that makes many anti-SJWs uncomfortable, but it is important to understand that what distinguishes us from the SJWs is not the type of air we breathe or the sort of tactics upon which we rely, but our ultimate objectives. Those ends do not justify the means, nor do they need to do so, as the means are fully justified by our enemy's use of them. The ends simply serve to make it perfectly clear that we are not them and they are not us. The reason the Germans did not use gas in World War II after introducing it in World War I was not because they had become more civilized, but because the French and British responded in kind. It is the ultimate purposes for which the tactics are used that matter, not the tactics themselves.

## Strategy 1: Build alternative institutions.

The long, slow, and insidious process of invading an institution, then gradually taking it over before steering it to serve one's own ends is not the sort of thing that comes naturally to the normal, honest individual. The amount of deception involved, combined with the considerable patience required, means that simply recreating the SJWs' long Gramscian march through the institutions of the West is not a viable solution. A better strategy, and one that is far more in line with our strengths, is building alternative institutions that will compete with the SJW-infested ones. This is a winning strategy due to the aforementioned Impossibility of Social Justice Convergence; their institutions have to serve the interests of social justice first, whereas our alternative institutions can focus solely on their primary functions.

Of course, it will be absolutely vital to design safeguards, the most powerful of which is a decentralized structure, into these institutions in order to keep SJWs out. One example of this is homeschooling, which is the rapidly growing institution that is competing very effectively with the SJW-infested traditional education system, so much so that the state of North Carolina recently announced that more children are being homeschooled than attend private schools; the number of North Carolina homeschoolers has increased 27 percent in just the last two years. Due to its intrinsically decentralized structure, homeschooling is a much more antifragile, much more SJW-resistant alternative to public schools than the private schools are, which is one reason that it is exploding in popularity around the world.

Homeschooling is the most important of these alternative institutions that will bring about the end of the SJWs in the long run, but there are many other cultural institutions that desperately need alternatives as well. Wikipedia is at the top of my personal list, as it is both extraordinarily influential and exceedingly vulnerable. It is influential because it is the first place that practically everyone in the media begins their research. It is vulnerable because as an open-source project, its current offering can easily be forked, and because its SJW affiliation is maintained by a mere 562 volunteer admins, half of one percent of whom are camped on my page.

Considering that as Supreme Dark Lord of the Evil Legion of Evil, I already have more than 430 Vile Faceless Minions at my beck and call, developing a machine language-enhanced alternative that is focused on providing all the true and relevant facts to the public rather than pushing the SJW Narrative across a wide range of subjects is a perfectly viable project. While it is true that past attempts to set up alternatives to Wikipedia have repeatedly failed, that does not mean that the task is impossible, and indeed, logic strongly suggests that someone will eventually succeed in creating one.

There are many other viable opportunites to create alternative SJW-free institutions as well. Technology is creating opportunities for disruption in many institutions. For example, Khan Academy is disrupting elementary and high school education while MIT's OpenCourseWare shows how higher education can be disrupted. It will take time, but the inability of the SJW-infested institutions to perform their primary functions means that the development of these alternative institutions is inevitable.

## Strategy 2: Reject their ideals.

Prior to the fall of the Soviet Union and the publication of *The Black Book of Communism: Crimes, Terror, Repression*, which chronicled that terrible ideology's ghastly historical body count, it was common for people to say that communism was a beautiful ideal, albeit one that had never been implemented properly. This was complete nonsense, of course, primarily driven by ignorance combined with a desire to avoid conflict with the Left without actually accepting its tenets.

In like manner, many people opposed to the lunatic behavior of the SJWs still mouth platitudes in support of the ideals of social justice. This is also a mistake. The way the core SJW tenets supposedly operate in theory are so observably divergent from reality that social justice could reasonably be regarded as a single massive experiment demonstrating the cognitive bias of individuals who erroneously believe themselves to be superior on the basis of a mistaken belief in their own competence, a bias known as the Dunning-Kruger effect.

Consider the four primary ideals of social justice: Equality, Diversity, Tolerance, and Progress. They are not even remotely complementary, as Equality and Diversity are mutually exclusive as well as standing directly in the way of Progress. How, for example, is Britain going to progress in any way when the results of the British embrace of equality and diversity have caused the average IQ of its 14-year-olds to fall two points from 1980 to 2008? Similar dyscivic effects have been observed in Denmark and in Australia. Indeed, how is the world going to progress if a scientific study published by the University of Hartford is correct and the average global IQ drops 8 percentage points in the next century? Social justice is not merely a mirage, it is an intrinsic self-contradiction.

The truth is that there is no such thing as equality. It does not exist in any physical, material, legal, philosophical, or spiritual sense. One might as usefully attempt to direct the entire efforts of a society's people and institutions towards the well-being of unicorns and fairies. As Martin van Creveld writes in *Equality: The Impossible Quest*, "Equality is a dream. When we keep in mind the costs that dream demands, the contradictions to which it inevitably leads, and the horrendous amounts of blood that are so often shed in its name, we would be wise to ensure that the quest for it does not become a nightmare".

Or better yet, abandon it altogether.

As for diversity, it is an intrinsic force for societal upheaval and collapse; as Heartiste has aptly stated the equation, Diversity + Proximity = War. And as was already pointed out in Chapter Six, Robert Putnam's "E Pluribus Unum: Diversity and Community in the Twenty-first Century" demonstrated how diversity destroys communities by weakening trust, and reducing social capital and engagement levels within them.

Tolerance is little more than a cloak for SJW entryism; if the SJWs truly believed in it as the ideal they profess, then surely they would practice it themselves. They don't even pretend to do so, and neither should we.

And finally, regarding Progress, you must ask yourself the question: Progress towards what? Since the true SJW answer is towards more socialism, more speech policing, more thought control, and more SJW control of society and its institutions, then the rational response must always be no, hell no, not at any price!

Our ideals of Truth, Liberty, and Justice are not only sufficient, but they are considerably superior to the nonsensical ideals of social justice. The ideals of social justice are not virtues; they are evils in disguise. Reject them without hesitation, reject them without apology, and reject them in their entirety.

## Strategy 3: Defund and destroy their propaganda centers.

While homeschooling is effectively, if gradually, removing millions of children each year from the SJW brainwashing factories more commonly known as the public schools, even those children are still subject to a barrage of SJW propaganda from Disney, Nickelodeon, the advertising industry, Hollywood, the news media, and other information centers.

Who makes these things possible? You do. I do. It is the see-no-evil support of us, the non-SJWs, who fund the cultural dominance of the SJWs and make it possible through our entertainment choices. We are financially forging our own chains!

And we know beyond any shadow of a doubt, we have conclusive evidence, that our dollars matter. The SJWs desperately wanted to shut down Chick-Fil-A. They thought they had successfully shut down *Duck Dynasty*. But the market power of the Christians who supported those two non-SJW entities was too great for the SJWs to resist. Mel Gibson's *The Passion of the Christ* was a massive success despite the fact that the Hollywood establishment hated it and denied it conventional distribution. Mike Judge's *Idiocracy*, which may be the most politically incorrect film ever made, was denied distribution but has gone on to earn 20 times more in DVD rentals than it did at the box office.

Now, I'm not advising the formation of another Moral Majority or Parents Music Resource Center. Both of those organizations lost the public relations battle and completely failed in their objectives. But that was BGG, Before #GAMERGATE, and the lessons that #GAMERGATE has learned in slowly strangling *Gawker Media* and denying it advertising revenue can be applied equally effectively by other groups that are opposed to the SJW propaganda flooding Western culture.

The most important lesson of #GAMERGATE in this regard is that everything starts with you. There is a saying in #GAMERGATE that invariably confuses outsiders, "I am the Leader of GamerGate". This is an inside joke; it is a joke because we have no leaders, we reject the very concept of leaders, and if anyone were to seriously try to put himself forward as a leader, everyone would mock him mercilessly as a shill. But it's more than a joke. It is also a form of encouragement, because the unspoken message it contains is "I am the Leader of GamerGate and so can you!"

In #GAMERGATE, no one gives any orders. No one tells you what to do. You're just expected to look around, see what needs doing, and then do it. No one made Milo, Mike, and me the leaders of #GamerGate in Paris. We just decided to do it; now we're looking at holding another one in Barcelona because Kukuruyo and some Spanish GamerGaters are interested in arranging a meetup there.

So don't wait for anyone else to do anything. Talk to a few friends. Kick around a few ideas. Send a few emails. Create a few Twitter memes and see if the spark happens to catch anyone's interest. Don't expect your target to come tumbling down, just start the process. Whether you succeed or not—and remember that #GamerGate has had far more abortive ops and ineffective failures than successes—the point is that you have taken a stand and you have struck a blow. And because you have done so, someone else will do so as well. It's impossible to know which one action will turn out to be effective, just as it's impossible to know which straw will be the one to snap the camel's back. But you do know this: the only action that is completely ineffective is the one that is never taken.

Because SJWs are primarily dependent upon other people's money, that is a weak point that should always be your first target. Dig to discover where they are obtaining their money, then focus your efforts on the funding source to cut off the flow of funds to them. Sometimes this will require political pressure, as many SJW institutions receive state, local, or federal government funds. Sometimes private pressure and a persuasive word in the ear of the relevant executive will suffice. But regardless, remember that every journey requires an initial step, and no one can take that first step except you.

## Strategy 4: Deny them employment.

This is the strategic element that will likely prove most difficult for even the most serious anti-SJW to accept, but it is a necessary one. Remember that turnabout is fair play and striking back in kind is justice. This is a cultural

party, and one of the primary reasons truth, liberty, and
˷ being systematically eradicated from our society is that their defenders are unwilling to take the cultural war seriously and are reluctant to
take out the enemy's soldiers. Make no mistake: That fat little middle-aged
woman who potters around the organization making herself indispensable as
she issues those seemingly harmless little homilies about diversity and equality is your enemy, and she *will not hesitate* to destroy your livelihood if given
the opportunity.

It is entirely common for non-SJWs to need to keep quiet about their
politics, about their religious faith, and in some cases, even about their identities in order to keep their jobs. I don't have a single game credit to either
my given name or my best-known pen name since 2007 because the game
companies with whom I work prefer to avoid the inevitable flak they will take
from SJWs within and without the company simply for hiring me. It doesn't
cause me very much trouble because I have a long history and a lot of personal connections in the industry, but younger, less-experienced non-SJWs
can be much more easily black-balled.

And make no mistake, they are being black-balled by SJWs in the industry. Leigh Alexander of *Gamasutra* and Laralyn McWilliams, the Chief
Creative Officer at The Workshop Entertainment, publicly threatened one
young developer's career for defending what Alexander called "sexist argument" in May 2015. Nor was that the only example chronicled by Deep-
Freeze.

The problem is that when SJWs are actively seeking out those who challenge their Narrative and disemploying them or preventing them from getting hired while non-SJWs blithely permit SJWs to freely enter their organizations, the outcome is both predictable and inevitable. The only way to
reverse the trend is to start actively hunting SJWs, using every available legal means to disemploy them. While race, sex, age and sexual orientation
are protected classes, political affiliations are not. Attempts by Republicans

and conservatives to sue universities have repeatedly failed, despite massively incongruous hiring patterns that violate the statistical standards of disparate impact far more greatly than is normally required to interest the Equal Employment Opportunity Commission.

So, once you've discovered that a co-worker or an employee belongs to a political party that indicates SJW sympathies, or has a COEXIST bumper sticker, or regularly utilizes language that indicates he is an SJW, arrange to have him jettisoned at the earliest opportunity. Don't let any misguided sympathy hold you back. In the long term it is literally a case of you or him. Rest assured, jettisoning you won't cause an SJW to lose any sleep at all. To the contrary, it's the very sort of thing he will brag about to his friends for years. You don't need to take any sadistic pleasure in hunting SJWs (although you may well develop a taste for it), but you do need to do it nevertheless in self-defense of your own career.

## Strategy 5: Restrict their speech.

This is much more easily accomplished than it sounds. A little shake of the head and a few disapproving clicks of your tongue every time an SJW buzzword is utilized will suffice to cause most SJWs to retreat. The average individual is highly inclined to seek approval from others, and SJWs tend to be more eager to gain approval than most. In fact, many people who appear to be SJWs probably aren't genuine SJWs. It's only that they think they need to parrot the SJW-speak that is the cultural sea in which they swim in order to win the approval they are seeking. So flip the script on them. Every time someone is blathering on about the need for more of this in that, or about inclusiveness, diversity, or equality, communicate disapproval and rejection to them. You don't need to argue or start an argument, as non-verbal communication is often the most effective response. Fold your arms, look up at the sky and avoid their eyes, sigh heavily, and refuse to provide them with any conversational encouragement. The aim should be to convey the attitude that you're simply waiting for them to stop pestering you and go away.

And when they finally summon the nerve to ask you why you're not interested in listening to them, ask them, in an incredulous tone of voice, if they actually believe any of that nonsense. Two times out of three, they'll deny it. That's the rhetorical advantage we have vis-a-vis the SJWs; our rhetoric is actually in line with objective, observable reality. Theirs is not. They have to lie because their worldview is in direct conflict with the world as it actually exists.

You should no more pretend to take seriously an SJW lying to you about equality or any other SJW tenet than you would if he was telling you about the giant pink elephant that he rode to work that day. In fact, treat any SJW assertion in exactly the same way you would a claim about a commute by pink pachyderm: with disbelief and ridicule. While the hardcore SJW will only retreat and wait for an opportunity to attack you, less committed SJWs and those who are only parroting the party line out of fear or habit will rapidly abandon it.

Eventually, it will become as problematic to speak positively about diversity as it is to praise racism now, and it will sound as ludicrous to claim a belief in equality as it would to assert one's opinion that there is, in fact, a pot of gold at the end of the rainbow.

## Strategy 6: Keep them out of your organizations.

I touched on the importance of keeping SJWs out of your organization in the section of the previous chapter that dealt with securing your base, but I didn't go into any detail describing how to do it. But if your goal is to prevent your organization from being infiltrated by SJWs over time, your approach will have to be structural, objective, and resistant to change. Relying upon individuals will always fail, sooner or later, because individuals are replaced and SJWs are known to be good at concealing their true ideals until they reach positions of power.

Robert Conquest, the great anti-Communist historian, articulated three laws of politics, two of which are relevant here.

- Any organization not explicitly right-wing sooner or later becomes left-wing.

- The simplest way to explain the behavior of any bureaucratic organization is to assume that it is controlled by a cabal of its enemies.

In light of these two political laws, it is advisable to look at two institutions that have proved considerably more resistant to infiltration and cooption than most: the Roman Catholic Church and the U.S. Army Rangers. We can also see, on the basis of the relative weakening of their resistance in recent years, what elements proved more important than others in permitting them to resist infiltration.

In the case of the Catholic Church, the extreme level of commitment required—lifetime celibacy—the length of the novitiate, and the time it takes to reach a position of authority, combined with the existence of a written text defining the organization's purpose, helped protect the Church against being coopted by its enemies, despite the many attempts by kings and emperors to do so over the centuries. Not until the Second Vatican Council, a revolutionary council that led to a widespread series of changes which dramatically weakened the Church as well as changed its orientation, did the Church begin to fall to its infiltrators. And while I am neither a Catholic nor well-versed in the details of Church history, when one examines the long list of post-Vatican II changes compiled by MyCatholicSource.com, a few tend to leap out immediately.

- New Canon Law

- New Catechism

- New Educational System

- Relaxation of Rules

- Elimination of Discipline

- Focus on Unity at the Expense of Truth

- Shift in Emphasis from Truth to Feelings

- Reliance on Lay "Experts"

- Conformity to the World

Sounds familiar, doesn't it? Upon reviewing the list, it is readily apparent that the SJWs successfully attacked the Catholic Church long before they got around to science fiction, let alone video games. Which makes sense; a Pope is far more dangerous than a mere writer or video game designer. So, the example of the Catholic Church provides the obvious lesson that those who target an organization's traditions, want to modify or otherwise bring them up to date, and appeal to outside standards to justify their calls for change are the very SJWs who need to be purged from the organization at the earliest opportunity.

While the U.S. military in general, and the U.S. Army Rangers in particular, have been targeted by feminists for decades, the so-called "point of the spear" remains remarkably unadulterated by social justice, in part because few SJWs are inclined to put themselves in physical danger, and in part because the military still requires highly skilled soldiers who are capable of killing people and breaking things without being troubled by concerns about Equality and Diversity. Tolerance is not a battlefield virtue.

The interesting thing is that despite the best efforts of SJWs in the military to push women into combat and the special forces, their efforts have largely failed due to the high level of physical standards involved. For example, not until 2012, when the standards for the Ranger Assessment and Selection Program were relaxed and 91 out of 114 soldiers graduated (an 80 percent pass rate that considerably exceeded the historical 30 percent rate), was it feasible to even think about female Rangers. Three years after the standards were relaxed, two women made U.S. Army Ranger history by passing the once-notoriously difficult Ranger School on their third try. And while the Rangers remain a formidable fighting force for the time being, we know, from the Impossibility of Social Justice Convergence, that it is only a matter of time before its ability to perform its primary function will be degraded.

But the example of the Rangers makes clear that the combination of unpleasant tasks and high objective standards is also an effective means of keeping SJWs out of an organization. And, as before, it is apparent that SJWs inside the organization can be easily identified as those who insisted on the need to relax those standards by appealing to social justice ideals.

In light of the observed experience of the Roman Catholic Church, the Rangers, and other institutions such as the universities, foundations, and Protestant churches that have been considerably less successful in resisting infiltration and cooption, SJW-proofing your organization should be built around the following concepts:

- A strong written constitution or statement of purpose focused on specific *material* objectives.

- Difficult objective standards for membership and leadership.

- A structured, scripted, and recorded interview process designed to unmask infiltrators.

- Strict procedural rules making rapid or extensive change as difficult as possible.

- Challenging and unpleasant tasks that the membership must regularly perform in order to maintain active membership that permits them a voice in the organization.

- Strict discipline combined with specified penalties up to and including expulsion.

- A regular ritual of renewal of loyalty to the organization and its objectives, on pain of expulsion.

- A requirement for all leaders and board members to have been members for at least 20 years.

- An internal affairs group responsible for ideologically policing the general membership but not the board or leadership. (This group is both the most useful and the most dangerous, as it is the best way to keep SJWs out as well as the first group that will be targeted by SJW entryists.) Only retired leaders and board members should be given this level of responsibility.

- A set of rules reserved to the leadership permitting and encouraging them to expel members who advocate substantive changes to the organization's primary objectives, bylaws, membership requirements, or disciplinary actions.

These are general principles, and no doubt you can think of other, more specific structural measures that will reduce the likelihood and effectiveness of SJW entryists which are more relevant to your specific type of organization. But the single most important principle to adopt is a ruthless intolerance for anyone expressing even a modicum of sympathy for social justice ideals. While this may sound too paranoid or detail-oriented for you, rest assured that if you do not go to the trouble of aggressively keeping out the SJWs, they will invade your organization, and they will do their best to take it over.

One pastor of a Southern Baptist church told me of an attempt on the church my wife and I attended prior to our arrival there. Over the course of several years, a number of families joined the church and became very active in it. Thanks to their enthusiastic support, one or two were soon invited to join the board of elders, which they gradually packed with their co-conspirators. They then tried to modify the church bylaws to place the pastor, who had started the church, under the direction of the board. The pastor managed to rally enough support to defeat their efforts and force them to resign from the board, but when the defeated infiltrators left the church, they took nearly a third of the membership with them.

Later, he learned that the same group of individuals had previously tried to pull the same stunt at two other churches, and were actively engaged in their fourth attempt.

It doesn't take much change for SJWs to enter en masse through the newly opened gates. Consider the SJW takeover of the Science Fiction Writers Association. Its transformation from a professional writers association defending the interests of science fiction writers to an SJW ancillary of Tor Books handing out awards to romance novels that may or may not take place in space was made possible by two changes. The size and makeup of the association was changed considerably after Anne McCaffrey threatened to quit unless her fantasy writer friends were permitted to join as well. And professional roots of the association were severed when the requalification requirement to publish one novel every five years in order to remain an active voting member was dropped. This allowed hundreds of amateur writers who had somehow managed to get one novel or three short stories published in the various qualifying small presses and magazines to stay active in the association, which they came to dominate over time. Rather like the old joke about the Holy Roman Empire being neither holy, nor Roman, nor an empire, SFWA now mostly consists of people who don't write for a living and are not particularly interested in science or science fiction.

# Strategy 7: Stay inside their OODA loops.

Col. John Boyd was a fighter pilot who transformed a dogfighting concept into a general principle of war that is well-known throughout the U.S. military. One of the most influential military strategists of the 20th century, he never wrote a book, but his *Discourse on Winning and Losing* presentation, in particular his concept of the OODA loop, which is the continuous cycle of engagement with one's environment, became famous in military circles. This cycle of engagement consists of four elements:

- Observation: the collection of data by means of the senses

- Orientation: the analysis and synthesis of data to form one's current mental perspective

- Decision: the determination of a course of action based on one's current mental perspective

- Action: the physical playing-out of decisions

Boyd's insight was that the speed with which one pilot could run through the cycle was the most important factor in separating victory from defeat. He also believed, as do many of his students, that this principle can be applied to a wide range of fields of competitive human endeavor, including business, sports, and politics. It makes sense, of course, that if you are acting while your opponent is still deciding on his course of action, or better yet, still trying to get himself oriented, you have both the initiative and the advantage, and therefore your chances of winning are better than his.

The idea, therefore, is to operate faster than your opponent, or to "stay inside his OODA loop". This means that by the time he has observed and reoriented himself to your previous action and is deciding what to do about it, you are hitting him again and resetting his cycle. This is a powerful conceptual tool because not only does it increase your chances of victory, but it tends to paralyze and demoralize your opponent. When your enemy is occupied with wondering when and where you are going to hit him next, he is not engaged in effective action of his own.

In practice, this means that not every attack needs to be well-planned or effective. The mere fact that you are hitting him elsewhere while he is still responding to your previous attack is likely to discombobulate and demoralize him. For example, the Tor boycott declared by Peter Grant has not, to the best of my knowledge, been materially effective in damaging Tor Books; they have not yet fired either Irene Gallo or Patrick Nielsen Hayden, at any rate. But the psychological effect it had on the SJWs of science fiction, coming as it did while they were still reeling from the shock of the Rabid Puppies near-sweep of the Hugo nominations, was out of proportion to its material effects. And, as the quote from Charles Stross at the front of the book indicates, the SJWs are now in a jumpy, paranoid state, wondering if our next attack will be on the Nebula Awards, the employment of an SJW editor, or somewhere else that they have not yet imagined.

As it happens, we already have multiple targets selected, and you can probably figure out what they are next year by listening for the shrieks of outraged science fiction SJWs. Since Rabid Puppies is, like #GamerGate, decentralized, even I don't know what all of them are, but I'm looking forward to finding out.

Although there are some military strategists, such as my *Riding the Red Horse* co-editor, LTC Tom Kratman, Ret. USA, a former Ranger who is more than a little dubious about the legitimacy of applying an Air Force doctrine to ground combat, there is no question that speed of decision-making and action have tended to go hand-in-hand with victory since Alexander the Great was chasing the King of Persia across Asia. From Hannibal and Julius Caesar to Napoleon, Heinz Guderian, Erwin Rommel, and George Patton, the most successful generals have tended to be more or less synonymous with speed.

So don't hesitate. Seize the initiative and always combine speed with audacity. Audacity alone is not enough though. After all, Georges Danton, the man famous for saying *"Audace, audace, et toujours de l'audace"*, ended up losing his head to the guillotine.

## Strategy 8: Punch back twice as hard.

This was the motto of the late Andrew Breitbart, and in his memory it has been adopted as a slogan by some of the more effective and combative individuals on the social media right, most notably Glenn Reynolds of Instapundit. It is a more succinct version of the Chicago Way advocated by Sean Connery in *The Untouchables*: "They pull a knife, you pull a gun. He sends one of yours to the hospital, you send one of his to the morgue."

SJWs are winning the cultural war because no one has been fighting them. No one has been resisting them. But now you know why you need to resist them. Now you know why you need to defeat them. And, most importantly, now you know how to do it.

For every sly little remark, speak back twice as hard. For every attempt at speech-policing, silence back twice as hard. For every attempt at isolation, shun back twice as hard. For every attempt to discredit, expose back twice as hard. For every attempted disemployment, fire back twice as hard. And for every lie, speak the truth twice as hard, twice as loud, and twice as long.

Show them no mercy because they do not believe in it and they do not deserve it.

> *The days of sitting on the fence and not opposing social justice warrior censorship because you don't agree with everything that (insert controversial figure) says are gone. It's shit or bust. It's free speech or no speech and it's time to pick a side.*
>
> —Paul Joseph Watson

# Chapter 10

# HOW TO TALK TO SJWS

*May I be allowed to finish? Sorry, I'm talking about men, darling.*

—Milo Yiannopoulos

After reading the previous chapters, you might well ask yourself why anyone in his right mind would ever want to talk to SJWs. But the fact is that you're going to have to do it sooner or later. Like most normal individuals you're probably going to find it difficult to talk to them, not only because they lie so frequently, but also because they genuinely do not hear what you think you are telling them.

This chapter is going to be a little more difficult than the previous chapters, but I encourage you to bear down and stick with it because the information it contains is the foundation upon which everything that preceded it was built. Nearly everything I have observed about SJWs can ultimately be traced back to a very important observation made by one of Man's greatest thinkers more than 2,337 years ago.

A few of the terms I am using here are esoteric and may be confusing, especially if you have encountered alternative uses of them before, but don't worry about the unfamiliar words; just concentrate on how the concepts being explained here apply to your interactions with SJWs today. And if you are familiar with other applications of these terms, remember that these are their original usages. These philosophical terms are used here in the sense of the original meanings that were later twisted, and in some cases, redefined to mean something completely different. Also, I should mention for the sake of those who know the subject better than I do that I am cutting a few corners here in order to keep it simple.

In his book *Rhetoric*, which is said to be "the most important single work on persuasion ever written", the Greek philosopher Aristotle divides the art of persuasion into two distinct forms, dialectic and rhetoric, concerning which he makes a very important observation. I can't stress enough how vital this observation is or how helpful it is to make the effort to understand it and take it to heart:

> *Before some audiences not even the possession of the exactest knowledge will make it easy for what we say to produce conviction. For argument based on knowledge implies instruction, and there are people whom one cannot instruct.*

"There are people whom one cannot instruct." One of Man's greatest thinkers, a brilliant teacher who tutored one of history's greatest generals, Alexander the Great, knew that there were people even he could not teach. He didn't say it was difficult to get through to them and he didn't say it would take a long time to instruct them, he concluded that it could not be done—at least not with mere knowledge.

However, he went on to point out that it is possible to convince them to change their minds, only that one cannot do so by presenting them with knowledge. Instead, it is necessary to manipulate them and to play upon their emotions in order to get them to change their minds. He even provided detailed instructions on how to go about communicating with these people who make decisions on the basis of their feelings rather than their logical capacities.

As you can probably guess, SJWs fall squarely into the category of people who cannot be instructed and cannot be convinced by knowledge. This is the key to understanding their astonishing ability to cling to their Narrative in the face of evidence that obliterates it as well as their insistence on clinging to it even as it shifts and contradicts itself. The reason SJWs can believe seven impossible and mutually contradictory things before breakfast is their inability to be instructed by knowledge; as long as each of those seven things happens to be in line with whatever their emotions are at the moment, SJWs will not see the inherent contradictions that thinking people do.

Because they do not think using logic, they cannot speak, or understand, what Aristotle describes as dialectic. Dialectic is based on the construction of logical syllogisms, which therefore makes it very easy to anyone who is capable of following those syllogisms and ascertaining their validity to detect when one is lying. Rhetoric, on the other hand, is "the faculty of observing in any given case the available means of persuasion". Rhetoric is much more forgiving of falsehood, and in fact, it's not even strictly possible to say that a rhetorical statement is a lie. Rhetoric consists of the construction of what Aristotle describes as enthymemes—which are not proper logical syllogisms, but incomplete or invalid arguments that merely take the form of syllogisms—in which all that matters is that persuasion is achieved by means of the "proof" provided, or more accurately, the apparent proof.

For the purposes of following this vital philosophical distinction, it might be easier to think in terms of "logically sound" and "not logically sound" rather than in simple terms of true and false. The point is that you can construct a logical syllogism that proves or a pseudo-logical enthymeme that *apparently* proves, but in either case, they can both be used to correctly point the person with whom you are speaking towards the relevant truth of the matter.

Let me give you a practical example of how this works. If I say "SJWs occasionally lie" in response to an SJW's false statement, this is proper dialectic but poor rhetoric, as it is likely to fail to persuade a rhetoric-speaker of the actual truth, namely, that the SJW is lying in the present circumstance. The better rhetorical statement is "SJWs always lie", which is not dialectically sound (or if you prefer, untrue), but despite its lack of soundness, it is more likely to persuade the rhetoric-speaker to believe the relevant truth, which is that the SJW is lying.

Hence the importance of knowing your audience and understanding which language of discourse they speak. When you speak in rhetoric to a dialectic-speaker, you will tend to sound very dishonest even when you are utilizing effective rhetoric that is perfectly in line with the truth. On the other hand, you can't speak dialectic to a rhetoric-speaker for the obvious reason that he cannot be informed or persuaded by it. He simply does not have the capacity.

I strongly prefer communicating in dialectic myself, but that is a language reserved for those who are intellectually honest and capable of changing their minds on the basis of information. So, I speak dialectic to those capable of communicating on that level, and I speak rhetoric to those who are not. Recall that rhetoric, to which SJWs are uniformly limited, is based not on logic or reason, but emotion. However, because many SJWs attempt to cloak their rhetoric in pseudo-dialectic, you can use sound dialectic to strip them of that pseudo-dialectic cloak on behalf of those capable of following the real thing, while communicating directly in rhetoric to the SJWs. This requires a degree of fluency in both discourse-languages as well as the ability to switch back and forth between them at will, a skill that takes some time to develop.

For example, consider the title of this book. It is not strictly true, in the dialectical sense, to assert that SJWs never tell the truth. To be dialectically sound, one should say, "SJWs frequently lie", or better yet, "SJWs have often been observed to lie in situations when doing so will serve their immediate interests". But as Aristotle tells us, the best rhetoric is rooted in truth, and the statement "SJWs always lie" rings emotionally true because SJWs lie so often, and so reliably, that it resonates with every individual who has been witness to their habitual dishonesty. That is why "SJWs always lie" is flawed dialectic, but accurate and effective rhetoric.

The interesting thing about rhetoric is that it makes very little sense to individuals who are limited to the dialectic. In fact, I didn't fully grasp the way it worked until reading *Rhetoric* for the second time. It can be bewildering when people tell you that they have been convinced by something that you know can't possibly have logically persuaded them to change their minds. In such cases, you know they have been persuaded by rhetoric, not facts, reason, or logic. And you should probably communicate with them through rhetoric in the future if you want them to understand you. When you speak dialectic to a rhetoric-speaker, he hears it as rhetoric. Or, not infrequently, as complete gibberish.

Dialectic and rhetoric are two different languages, and the number of people who can speak both of them fluently is relatively small. I wouldn't expect an individual who only speaks one form of discourse to be any more able to follow me into the other se passo a scrivere in italiano o francese senza preavviso dopo l'inizio di una frase in inglese. Il est déroutant quand quelqu'un se coupe subitement langues sur vous, nicht wahr?

In case it is not already apparent, this chapter is primarily written for dialectic-speakers. Rhetoric-speakers, especially SJWs who are inclined to think badly of me, will only see "blah blah blah, Aristotle, blah blah blah, I'm so smart, blah blah blah, spaghetti spaghetti" and scan through what looks like nothing but a word salad to them trying to find something they can use to minimize or disqualify me.

And that is *exactly* what an SJW does to you whenever you are trying to communicate with him using logic, reason, and knowledge. Have you ever had an experience where you have clearly laid out a complete train of thought for someone, only to have him stubbornly declare that you are wrong, that you must be wrong, and there is no possibility you could be correct, and doing so without pointing to a single flaw anywhere in your argument? You were speaking the wrong language. You were speaking in dialectic to a rhetoric-speaker, and it didn't work, did it?

Even SJWs who can more or less understand dialectic don't speak it themselves. That is why they are infamous for never admitting they are wrong even when everyone else can see it, and why they are constantly moving the goalposts and revising the history of what everyone knows actually happened. It is absolutely pointless to speak in dialectic to them; unless you are actually talking to them for the benefit of an audience, there is no reason not to go directly to rhetoric and hammer on their emotions rather than relying on reason to accomplish the impossible.

Consider the following exchange that took place on Twitter with an SJW from the game industry in light of what you've learned regarding SJWs, dialectic, and rhetoric. To put the discussion into context, it may help to know that Palle Hoffstein is a German SJW who is the Creative Director for Blue Byte, an Ubisoft-owned studio. Mark Kern, aka Grummz, is a highly respected game designer who is the founder of Red 5 Studios and League 4 Gamers but is best known for having been the team lead for *World of Warcraft* while at Blizzard. He has an impressive list of development credits that, in addition to *World of Warcraft*, includes massively successful games such as *Starcraft* and *Diablo 2*. I am a longtime game industry veteran who was a nationally syndicated game reviewer and a contributor to *Computer Gaming World*, and I have worked with Intel, Creative Labs, THQ, Sega, GT Interactive, and Funcom, among others, as a lead or senior designer. Both Grummz and I have been in the industry for more than two decades, while Hoffstein has credits dating back to 1998. American McGee is a well-known lead designer with whom I have been acquainted since he was a level designer working on *Doom II: Hell on Earth.*

At the time, Mark Kern was not a GamerGater, although he was known to be sympathetic to #GAMERGATE, and three months later he announced, to widespread approval: "That is F()&#$%king it! I AM NOW #GAMERGATE !!!!!" That being said, the fact that Kern was not a GamerGater at the time of this exchange is significant because it highlights the First Law of SJW in action.

In the discussion below, I have indicated rhetoric in bold and observably false statements in strikethrough.

Palle Hoffstein

**Grummz and Vox are "the future of gaming" apparently.**

Palle Hoffstein

*Gaters in my mentions defending Kern.* ***~~For a leaderless group they sure love their leaders.~~***

Palle Hoffstein

*Also Kern is now chiming in on the Hugo awards, ~~another thing he knows nothing about.~~*

Palle Hoffstein

*So Mark Kern is getting chummy with Vox Day? I suppose it was just a matter of time.*

*Mark Kern retweeted*

*Vox Day Apr 2*

*American McGee's criticism of SJW characters in games is similar to my criticism of them in SF/F books.*

University Watch

*So if you are going to say spiteful things about @voxday and @Grummz* #SAYITTOTHEIRFACE *Palle.* #GAMERGATE

Palle Hoffstein

~~*I have spoken to them many times.*~~ **Settle down.**

Vox Day

*When have you ever spoken to me? I'm afraid I don't recall.*

Palle Hoffstein

~~*Twitter. A while ago.*~~ ~~**Not that memorable for me either.**~~

Vox Day

*So once on Twitter is "many times"? Look, if you've got criticism, that's fine.* **The line is over there.**

Palle Hoffstein

*I wasn't the one who tagged you.* ~~*I was talking about Kern.*~~ **If I feel the need I will address you directly, I assure you.**

Vox Day

*No, you were talking about me. And you have not talked to me many times. So you've lied and tried to dissemble.* **Why?**

Palle Hoffstein

*Look Vox, I didn't tag you. I didn't want to talk to you.* **I can't imagine anyone ever wants to talk to you. Buzz off.**

Vox Day

*No, you wanted to talk ABOUT me.* **I would think as a game designer, you would get how this "social media" thing operates.**

Dave Injustice

@Palle_Hoffstein *for someone not talking to someone, you sure spend a lot of time talking about them*

Notice that the majority of Hoffstein's statements are rhetorical and are intended to provoke emotion rather than to communicate information. In only eight tweets, he tells six provable lies and offers up two attempts at misdirection. (It's technically true that he didn't "tag" me, but the relevant point he is evading there is that he was the one responsible for bringing me up in the first place.) The most glaring SJW tell in this exchange is when Hoffstein, having been caught red-handed lying about his claim to have talked to Mark Kern and me "many times", doesn't back down and admit it, but instead resorts to pseudo-dialectical rhetoric combined with pure rhetoric in order to try to spin the Narrative and to retain his pose of superiority. Because he was a game dev talking down to gamers, he was not only caught out, he was also caught off-guard by suddenly having to deal with someone who is more or less at his level of status in the industry. And so we see both the First and Second Laws of SJW at work, as well as the SJW's expected rhetorical response to dialectic.

My statement is pure dialectic; it is nothing but raw information. Although I have had some dealings with Ubisoft, it was with two different studios, I did not recall ever having spoken with Hoffstein, and I was pretty sure I never had. Later, I went back through my Twitter account and was able to verify that contra Hoffstein's assertion, he had never spoken to me, and I had never spoken to him either. I also asked Mark Kern if he had ever spoken to Palle Hoffstein. He could not remember ever having done so but did recall once exchanging a pair of tweets with him. However, according to Twitter Advanced Search, this exchange took place two months *after* Hoffstein claimed to have spoken to both of us "many times".

SJWs always lie.

As for Hoffstein's response, it is part false pseudo-dialectic ("Twitter. A while ago"), and part pure rhetoric intended to try to invoke a negative emotion in me ("Not that memorable for me either"). This is very typical. Because the SJW cannot speak dialectic, he will attempt to intimidate the person with whom he is speaking through rhetorical posturing. This is why, when pressed, SJWs invariably either run away or resort to shrieking angry insults that often don't even make any sense in the context of the conversation.

The correct strategy is to fight dialectic with dialectic, expose pseudo-dialectic with dialectic, and fight rhetoric with rhetoric. And the most important thing about implementing that strategy is to understand that with rhetoric, the actual information content is largely irrelevant.

Rhetoric is all about what emotions you trigger in the other person; when SJWs talk to each other, they try to inflate themselves at the other's expense in order to sort out their position in the SJW hierarchy. Of course, SJW metrics are all but unintelligible to normal, sane human beings, so it can be amusing as well as educational to watch them attempt to simultaneously exaggerate both their importance and their victimhood. The perfect Queen of the SJWs—and she would be a queen, never a king—would be a mixed-race lesbian Swedish immigrant who was abused as a child by a conservative white Republican politician and kept as a sex slave by neo-Nazis with Confederate-flag tattoos prior to writing a bestselling novel about a fictionalized version of her terrible experiences, appearing on Oprah, and starring on a science fiction TV show popular with white nerds.

The basic idea is that if you can make the other person feel small or angry, you are winning at SJW rhetoric. This is why SJWs are constantly accusing other people of being mad or upset; it's just another way of them claiming to be winning the conversation. If you can make the other person submit, run away, or fall silent, then you have won the conversation, and you are higher in the SJW hierarchy than he is. So it doesn't matter what you actually say, and in fact, resorting to straight-up namecalling, the more ridiculous the better, is often the fastest and most efficient way to get through the conversational process with an SJW. If he launches the usual "sexist, racist, homophobic, Nazi" line, don't blink and don't defend yourself. Just hit him right back with "racist, child molester, pedophile, monster" and watch him run. If you're of a more delicate constitution and are not willing to go that far even when attacked unprovoked, try "creepy" and "stalker" on the men and "psycho" or "ugly" on the women. This will usually have much the same effect. You will know your rhetoric is effective when they block you online, or in person if their eyes widen with shock and their jaw drops. And you have mastered the art of rhetoric when you can make an SJW retreat in tears or cause a room full of people to gasp in disbelief before bursting out laughing at the SJW.

Again, you must keep in mind that the actual information content is irrelevant. SJWs communicate in competitive emotion. If you're not doing the same, then you're not communicating with them, you're doing little more than serving as a punching bag for their verbal strikes. I realize this probably doesn't make sense, but that is because you are a normal, sane individual who thinks rather than feels. But keep in mind that just as their argument "X is Not X because feelbad" makes no sense to you, your argument that "X cannot be Not X due to the law of non-contradiction" makes no sense to an SJW.

Don't try to work through the logic of it all. Just try it. It works. Chances are that you'll be as surprised as I was to discover how effective it can be to speak in rhetoric to the rhetoric-speakers. When Milo Yiannopoulos destroyed a feminist on live television during a public debate concerning modern Britain's hostility to men, it wasn't his smooth recitation of relevant facts that left her reeling in shock and disarray; she blithely ignored all of that. It was his dismissive use of the word "darling" that literally muted her. Her wide, staring eyes and gaping mouth made it very clear how powerful a well-placed, well-timed rhetorical bomb can be.

Ironically, if you do respond to them in their own rhetorical language, SJWs will not only better understand you but may even express an amount of begrudging appreciation for your mastery of it. Consider this purely rhetorical exchange that took place with a pair of SJWs who were attempting to convince me to abandon my support for Roosh, and thereby increase the social pressure on him by isolating him. But instead of responding as they expected by either a) accepting their attempt to disqualify Roosh or b) taking the dialectical approach of resorting to the facts to defend Roosh against their false charges, I challenged their attempt to establish the Narrative by using rhetoric that redirected their disqualification attempt towards one of their fellow SJWs.

Notice, as you read it, that they're not offended by this and that they can't even bother to pretend to care about the supposedly serious criminal accusations being flung about. They are, however, quick to recognize that because I am utilizing their own form of rhetoric against them, there is no point attempting to put any further social pressure on me in this regard. Had I given in, they would have increased the pressure and demanded that I demonstrate my newfound purity of heart by publicly denouncing and disavowing Roosh. Had I tried to defend Roosh using dialectic, the exchange would have gone on for pages as they danced around all of the relevant facts and continued to turn up the rhetorical heat on me. But because they received a muscular response in their own rhetorical language, they were quickly convinced that their efforts were futile.

Brosephus Aurelius

*wait isnt Roosh that PUA sex tourist guide guy that offended a good chunk of europe with his books?*

Vox Day

*Straight to DISQUALIFY. Textbook SJW. Well done.*

Brosephus Aurelius

*I'm not disqualifying his opinion, just checking if you knew his past public exposure before linking. I'm still reading the link*

James Mathurin

*Don't forget he's also an admitted rapist.*

Vox Day

*No, that's John "I'm a rapist" Scalzi. You can even hear him admit it here:* (link to MP3)

James Mathurin

*Nah, it's Roosh.*

Vox Day

*That's a direct quote from 25 October 2012. You literally can't get any more "self-admitted rapist" than that.*

James Mathurin

*At some point, will you explain why you think I care? I was talking about Roosh V being an admitted rapist.*

Vox Day

*You've provided no evidence at all. I've provided conclusive proof that John Scalzi is a self-admitted rapist.*

Vox Day

*So, you are actually saying you don't care that John Scalzi is a self-admitted rapist. Wow just wow.*

Brosephus Aurelius

*11/10 wizard tier trolling*

"Trolling" is what SJWs call it when you reply to them in their own rhetorical language.

Remember that there is no truth content in emotion-based rhetorical speech. All that matters is for the emotion to be genuine in the moment. And that is why SJWs always lie. Because as long as they don't *feel* as if they're lying, they don't *believe* they are lying, regardless of what objective reality might have to say about the falsity of their assertions.

This connection between social justice warriors and emotion is neither a new nor an original observation. F.A. Hayek made the connection 40 years ago in *The Mirage of Social Justice* when he wrote, "The commitment to 'social justice' has in fact become the chief outlet for moral emotion, the distinguishing attribute of the good man, and the recognized sign of the possession of a moral conscience".

So, with support from the brilliant minds of Aristotle and Hayek, you can be assured that you are on sound intellectual ground when, instead of relying on information and dialectic to convince the SJWs with whom you are communicating, you focus on using rhetoric to manipulate their emotions and thereby their behavior.

# POSTSCRIPT

*Friends, remember that you are as honorable as the risk you take for your opinions.*

—Nassim Nicholas Taleb

The self-appointed thought police are everywhere. Yet we need not despair at the size of the monumental task that lies before us because we will eventually defeat them. Sooner or later, reality always tears through the veil of even the most powerful illusion. We have no need of numbers. One man armed with the truth will eventually overcome ten million preaching a lie. SJWs not only lie, but they are aware, on some instinctual level, that they are lying. That is the reason they defend their ever-mutating Narrative so ferociously. Even a modicum of the truth is enough to chip away at it. Even a single man who refuses to declare that there are five lights instead of four is a deadly threat to them, which is why not even an inkling of the truth can be tolerated by the SJWs, and why those who resist the SJW Narrative are attacked with such vengeance.

SJWs always lie. They are fundamentally in conflict with science, history, logic, and reality, and that is why they are doomed to defeat in the end. To defeat them, one need do nothing more than to stand resolutely by the truth as best you see it and by the truth-tellers you meet along the way. Battles will be lost, to be sure, and if history is any guide, telling the truth will always come at a cost, but in the long run, vindication and victory in the Social Justice War are inevitable for those who love truth and freedom.

# APPENDIX A

*On July 12, 2015, Mike Cernovich, Milo Yiannopoulos, and I hosted one of the 43 #GAMERGATE meetups that took place around the world during the first year of #GAMERGATE, GGinParis. It was a small event, with about 40 people, but it was a successful one despite several threats of disruptive violence being made on Twitter by anti-GamerGaters. It was covered by the French newspaper* Le Monde *as well as by the Paris journal* La Chasseur. *This was the speech I made during the event.*

First of all, thank you and welcome from Milo and Mike and I. Thank you all for coming. What I want to say is that what #GAMERGATE is doing is vastly important. Today, I read that Ellen Pao from *Reddit* was jettisoned, and what happened there would not have happened without #GAMERGATE. What #GAMERGATE has done is plant a seed. #GAMERGATE is the very first organization in decades that has stood up to the social justice warriors and said No! We will play what we want to play, we will develop what we want to develop, and we will design what we want to design!

It's not a political movement. I may be right-wing, some of you may be left-wing, but we're all in this together, saying that we have the right to do what we want and we have the right to do it no matter what anybody else thinks. So the three things that I want you to remember tonight are this:

First, what you're doing is important. Second, what you're doing is making a difference in other industries besides games. We're seeing people in science fiction, we're seeing people in technology, we're seeing people in comics, we're seeing people in movies, we're seeing people in television all standing up and saying no because they saw you do it.

And the third thing, the most important thing I want you to keep in mind, is that you're not alone. There is a small group of us here in Paris tonight, but there are groups of people meeting tonight in Dallas-Fort Worth and in Arlington, Virginia. There have been people gathering in Sydney, Australia, in Washington, D.C., in Utah, in California, and all around the world who are your brothers and sisters in this.

To #GamerGate around the world!

# APPENDIX B

*Milo Yiannopoulos was one of #GAMERGATE's representatives at the Airplay event in Miami hosted by the Society of Professional Journalists, but he never had the opportunity to finish his address because he was interrupted by the police evacuating the building after multiple bomb threats were phoned in. After writing the Foreword to this book, he asked me if he might have the final word as well, and since Milo always gets what he wants sooner or later, I figured I would save everyone time and just say yes right away. After reading it, I also realized it was something well worth including in this book for the sake of posterity and the public record.*

I'm Milo Yiannopoulos. I'm an author, broadcaster, journalist and satirist. I've been covering GamerGate closely, and I guess become part of the furniture since this time last year.

But there's one important thing that separates me from GamerGate, and it's not the accent or the hair.

It's my politics. Unlike the rest of GamerGate, I'm happy to admit I'm a pretty conservative guy. And I'd be lying if I said I didn't recognise the potential of GamerGate to give the Left a bloody nose when in August 2014 I was approached by Allum Bokhari, now my colleague at Breitbart, with the story.

But I quickly realised this wasn't a Left-Right thing at all. It's more about

nannying pearl-clutchers with bully pulpits in the media versus decent, ordinary people who just want to be left alone. Authoritarianism versus lib-
ertarianism, if you like. And the extraordinary lengths authoritarians will
sometimes go to in order to impose their will on others—even about something as apparently trivial as the humble video game.

GamerGate is wrongly called a conservative movement simply because
the only journalists willing to cover it fairly, or to give the movement time of
day, were classical liberals, for whom there is really no home in the modern
progressive left. That was another realisation that stung GamerGate supporters, who even now think of themselves as reflexively left-wing, despite what
the liberal media has done to them.

The fact is, I wouldn't be here if gaming journalism hadn't made me
necessary. I'm not a professional games critic. I'm a student, if you like,
of internet cultures. But there would have been no space for me in this
debate had the press covered this story fairly or responsibly. You might say my
position in GamerGate and reputation among gamers generally are creations
of *Kotaku* and *Polygon*.

GamerGate is remarkable—and attracts the interest of people like
me—because it represents perhaps the first time in the last decade or more
that a significant incursion has been made in the culture wars against guilt-
mongers, nannies, authoritarians, gender activists, faux academic bloggers
in places like *Gawker*, *Vox* and *Buzzfeed* and troublesome agitators of all de-
scriptions.

So that's what excited me originally. I didn't have it in for feminists or
anything like that—at least not really. But perhaps, mostly as a result of
GamerGate, I sort of do now.

Gamers have no social capital. In fact, it's worse than that: everyone
hates them. The Right hates gamers because it blames games for real-world
violence. The Left now hates them because progressives have come to accuse
video games, bizarrely, of somehow being able to make people sexist.

What makes this scandal on the one hand a great story but on the other genuinely tragic and upsetting is that it represents not a culture clash but a kind of geek civil war. The people on either side of this debate are remarkably similar, and closer to one another than either group is to the rest of us.

That's why it hurt GamerGate and anti-GamerGate to see their favourite celebrities start to pick sides. This was a family argument that became public and then escalated out of control.

But it was a family argument created by bad journalism. Bad journalism didn't just report on GamerGate in all the shoddy and unacceptable ways you've already heard about. Gaming journalism started the whole schism in the first place, by insulting and ridiculing readers and handing its moral compass over to highly questionable people with axes to grind and wacky activist politics designed to divide.

Then it drove a wedge down the middle of its own base of readers by cruelly, and in the absence of fact or justification, calling one side the most appalling names, while credulously, assiduously and reflexively supporting some of the most obviously and ostentatiously unreliable people in the history of journalistic sourcing.

Even worse, the war was precipitated by people who don't even play, or much care about, video games. Anita Sarkeesian admits, in footage you can find online but she'll never acknowledge, that she's not a gamer and doesn't particularly like video games. That story changed dramatically when she was given space in the *New York Times*. She suddenly remembered a whole childhood she'd previously forgotten about in which not only was she a GameBoy addict but she was also, implausibly, very much aware of how *Tetris* was, like, really male-oriented. Or something, who knows.

The people GamerGate calls "social justice warriors"—the feminist activists, bloggers and so on—annoy gamers in part because so few of them really give a damn about gaming. Some call themselves "developers" without having ever released anything of substance. The press doesn't know, and doesn't bother to find out, how credible these claims are.

When GamerGate gave birth to a now-infamous *Law and Order: Special Victims Unit* episode, it wasn't gamers who'd wet the bed. It was journalists. That hour of television did more to damage the image of the gaming industry than anything gamers had ever done. And the media made it happen.

It also reinforced the most persistent myth in all of this: that gaming is a terrible place for women to be. Now, I can't tell you the pathology that leads some of the most female and minority-friendly spaces in the world to become guilt-ridden and obsessed with diversity, quotas and inclusion.

But I've seen it before. I started my reporting career in the startup world—London and Silicon Valley—and the same is true of the Facebooks, Twitters and Snapchats of this world. They're some of the best places you could ever get a job as a woman. But for some reason the startup industry, just like gaming, is convinced that there's an epidemic of violent misogyny within it. It's just not true.

Yet that *Law and Order* episode gave the impression to women that gaming was a hostile place for them to be. Most women aren't strident gender activists brandishing placards and blog posts about micro-aggressions.

If they hear an industry is a terrible place to go for women, they'll simply quietly avoid it. That's what gaming journalism has achieved through a combination of negligence and malice: it has convinced the world that gaming is a scary place for a woman to be. I've received I would estimate between 50 and 100 emails from women, in gaming—female critics of the gender warriors—saying that's simply not the industry they wake up to every day.

So journalists are doubly responsible in the case of GamerGate, both for creating the situation in the first place and then constantly inflaming it.

Specifically, I think gamers were subjected to six unacceptable journalistic injustices.

1. The worst elements in GamerGate were taken as prima facie evidence of what the authentic heart of the movement was like. We don't do

that for any other movement, whether Occupy, Black Lives Matter or even, when you think about it, Islamic terrorism. Only GamerGate.

2. Worse, uniquely to GamerGate, there is no evidence that these "worst elements" were even part of the movement, had anything to do with it, knew any of the people driving the movement or believed in its objectives. Both sides have admitted that third-party trolls have been active throughout. But only anti-GamerGate is given the benefit of the doubt. Why?

3. GamerGate, again, uniquely in the history of hashtag movements, was never given the right to defend or define itself. We bend over backwards to describe Occupy and Black Lives Matter in terms acceptable to those movements—to give them self-determination and agency. That was denied to GamerGate because the subject at hand was press ethics, and journalists didn't want to admit they had a point.

4. Based on my year of reporting on this subject, I believe some journalists in the gaming industry actively suppressed evidence—facts they must have known about—in order to present a narrative that did not cohere with reality. They systematically ignored not just the stated objectives of the movement but evidence that GamerGate supporters were being subjected to bullying, harassment, doxxing, swatting, threats and even real-life intimidation. It's now well known that I received an unsheathed syringe, a dead animal and a razor blade in the mail. *Kotaku* had to be publicly shamed into acknowledging any of this. If my reporting had been sympathetic to the other side of the debate, it would have been headline news. For those who like to keep score, it's also worth remembering that the only bomb threat considered credible by the police in the history of GamerGate wasn't directed at Anita Sarkeesian, but against a well-mannered meetup of gamers I organised in Washington, D.C.

5. GamerGate victims have been subjected to a class war they didn't want and didn't start. Journalism is supposed to give a voice to the voiceless. In this instance it failed completely to identify the real victims and went on a crusade against an innocent party.

6. Finally, as we've seen from the GameJournoPros revelations, journalists actively conspired with one another to shift the Overton window dramatically on this subject, making it professionally dangerous simply to report facts, as they had been doing for a decade on related subjects. As journalists, we have a word for environments in which it is dangerous to report true facts or question the establishment consensus, don't we?

With GamerGate, Conservatives missed an opportunity to explore a new front in the culture wars because it didn't have the courage to consider whether its history of demonising video games might have been a mistake. And progressives screwed up by allowing narrative to triumph over fact. We've seen elsewhere—in *Rolling Stone*, the Duke Lacrosse case and the case of Mattress Girl Emma Sulkowicz, the devastating consequences that can have.

Journalists lost sight of who the powerful and who the powerless were in this debate. They mistook the double-speak and grievance culture of professional activists for women in need and accepted that a disproportionately male culture simply must have something wrong with it.

This shames our profession greatly. If the future of journalism is picking a side before the facts are in and wantonly, willfully, mercilessly bullying other people—if it's activism over fact-based reporting—then I'm out. I'll go be a comedian or a hair salon receptionist or something.

Great art asks questions. It provokes and challenges us.

Art is not circumscribed by one person's hurt feelings or opinion on what might be "harmful". All GamerGate is asking for is the right to pursue its own truth and, sure, its own pleasure, in its own way.

But when a small but tight-knit cabal of people, all of whom think identically, all of whom are determined to defame ordinary consumers and become professional nuisances to the industry they profess to love, the chilling effects can be devastating.

That's what happened here. And it's a testament to the extraordinary, brilliant resilience of gamers that a year on, despite every conceivable bad word being hurled at them, they remain unbowed. Today, they're asking you to look again.

Gaming culture is messy and sarcastic and full of bitching, banter, back-stabbing, memes and one-upmanship. It's also precious, fragile and desperately important for the many marginalised voices and people who depend on it for safety and security.

Some of those marginalised people don't look like you think they will. But that doesn't mean they don't rely on the culture they've built to sustain, nurture and protect them. Gaming culture is its own unique kind of safe space. And journalists should be exploring and celebrating that, not callously and mendaciously attempting to destroy it.

# APPENDIX C

The details concerning my pseudo-expulsion from the Science Fiction and Fantasy Writers Association are not relevant to the wider cultural war against the social justice warriors, nor do I feel any need to defend myself or justify my actions, but because the SJWs in science fiction will almost surely attempt to claim I am attempting to gloss over what took place if sufficient details are not provided, I have provided a factual summary in this appendix.

Not long after the SFWA election I lost to Steven Gould, an African-American fantasy writer named N.K. Jemisin was the guest of honor at a convention in Australia. She's one of the affirmative-action writers more talked about than read by science fiction's SJWs, who like nothing better than to prove their dedication to Diversity by nominating ideologically re-liable minorities for various awards regardless of how mediocre their works happen to be. Jemisin is an aggressive race-baiting lunatic who had pre-viously accused both Robert Heinlein and "most of SF fandom" of being "racist as *fuck*" before publicly attacking me, the countries of Australia, Japan, and Italy, the states of New York, Alabama, Florida, and Texas, and two elderly white male science fiction writers in her Guest of Honor speech at Continuum in June 2013.

In that speech, after announcing that her father had feared for her safety in racist Australia, complaining about racism in Japan, Italy, New York, and Alabama, complaining about the racism she had already experienced in her first two days in Australia, and declaring that laws in Florida and Texas permitted whites to shoot and kill people like her without consequence, she proceeded to blatantly lie about an individual who could only be me.

> *For the past few days I've also been observing a "kerfuffle", as some call it, in reaction to the Science Fiction and Fantasy Writers of America's latest professional journal,* the Bulletin. *Some of you may also have been following the discussion; hopefully not all of you. To summarize: two of the genre's most venerable white male writers made some comments in a series of recent articles which have been decried as sexist and racist by most of the organization's membership. Now, to put this in context: the membership of SFWA also recently voted in a new president. There were two candidates—one of whom was a self-described misogynist, racist, anti-Semite, and a few other flavors of asshole. In this election he lost by a landslide… but he still earned ten percent of the vote. SFWA is small; only about 500 people voted in total, so we're talking less than 50 people. But scale up again. Imagine if ten percent of this country's population was busy making active efforts to take away not mere privileges, not even dignity, but your most basic rights. Imagine if ten percent of the people you interacted with, on a daily basis, did not regard you as human.*

Instead of correctly dismissing Jemisin's speech as the ravings of a deranged professional victim, the SJWs in SFWA tearfully hailed it as a beautiful call to arms.

- *"I read that speech with tears in my eyes. Extremely moving and extremely important. I wish I had heard it in person. I urge every SFWA member to read it."* —Jason Sanford

- *"Excellent speech. One thing that shines through is that there's more to inclusivity than simply not being exclusive. I'd like to think that SFWA as a professional organization can be a safe space for its members, and this incident certainly adds weight to the arguments that SFWA isn't, currently, such an environment. Is this time to re-visit the question of a code of conduct again?"* —Charles Stross

Jemisin's attack on Mike Resnick, Barry Malzberg, and me was directly linked to in the official SFWA discussion forums by several SFWA members. This is significant for reasons that will shortly become clear. I responded with the following post, to which I linked using the @sfwaauthors feed on Twitter.

*NK Jemisin is publicly lying about me and a few other things in Australia as she blithely advocates the continued self-destruction of science fiction.*

*Let me be perfectly clear. I do not describe myself as a "misogynist, racist, anti-Semite, and a few other flavors of asshole". Jemisin has it wrong; it is not that I, and others, do not view her as human, (although genetic science presently suggests that we are not equally homo sapiens sapiens), it is that we simply do not view her as being fully civilized for the obvious historical reason that she is not.*

*She is lying about the laws in Texas and Florida too. The laws are not there to let whites "just shoot people like me, without consequence, as long as they feel threatened by my presence", those self-defense laws have been put in place to let whites defend their lives and their property from people, like her, who are half-savages engaged in attacking them.*

*Jemisin's disregard for the truth is no different than the average Chicago gangbanger's disregard for the traditional Western code of civilized conduct. She could, if she wished, claim that privileged white males are responsible for the decline of Detroit, for the declining sales of science fiction, even for the economic and cultural decline of the United States, but that would not make it true.*

*It would not even make it credible. Anyone who is paying sufficient attention will understand who is genuinely responsible for these problems.*

*Unlike the white males she excoriates, there is no evidence to be found anywhere on the planet that a society of NK Jemisins is capable of building an advanced civilization, or even successfully maintaining one without significant external support from those white males. If one considers that it took my English and Irish ancestors more than one thousand years to become fully civilized after their first contact with advanced Greco-Roman civilization, it should be patently obvious that it is illogical to imagine, let alone insist, that Africans have somehow managed to do the same in less than half the time at a greater geographic distance. These things take time.*

*Being an educated, but ignorant half-savage, with little more understanding of what it took to build a new literature by "a bunch of beardy old middle-class middle-American guys" than an illiterate Igbotu tribesman has of how to build a jet engine, Jemisin clearly does not understand that her dishonest call for "reconciliation" and even more diversity within SF/F is tantamount to a call for its decline into irrelevance. Nor do the back-patting Samuel Johnsons wiping their eyes and congratulating her for her ever-so-touching speech understand that.*

*There can be no reconciliation between the observant and the delusional.*

The SJWs in SFWA promptly went berserk. This was more than a challenge to their Narrative. It was a direct assault on one of their most sacred totems! Their problem was that I had not violated any rules of the organization in exercising my right of free speech to defend myself against Jemisin's false accusations on my own blog, so they produced an 80-page report that spent more time analyzing things other people said on other sites than it did about anything to do with me and tried to justify their attempt to expel me from the association on the basis of a single tweet made on an unofficial Twitter account. Ironically enough, I had absolutely NOT done what many other members, including the president-elect and two other board members had done, which was to attack or link to an attack on a fellow member in a space "sponsored by SFWA, including but not limited to the SFWA discussion Forums, the SFWA website, the Nebula Awards Weekend, and the SFWA suite".

This was easy for me to prove, as the Twitter terms of service made it clear that the Services belonged to Twitter while the Content of the tweet belonged to me. SFWA neither sponsored nor controlled @sfwaauthors or its content as @SFWA was the official account controlled by the association.

The report was so ineptly constructed, and so embarrassing to SFWA, that when I made it available to the public along with my 34-page response taking it apart section by section, the association's Operations Manager filed a DMCA takedown notice with me and with my ISP in order to bury it.

> *Kate Baker*
> *Date: August 19, 2013, 3:52:59 PM CDT*
> *Subject: DMCA Take-down Notice - Request*
>
> *Requester: Kathryn Baker - Operations Manager SFWA*
> *Organization: Science Fiction and Fantasy Writers of America*
> *On Behalf of Copyright Holder: Matthew Johnson - Regional Director - SFWA*
>
> *Work infringed - SFWA_report.pdf*
>
> *Title: Evidence regarding the complaints made against Theodore Beale*
> *Report to the Board of Directors of SFWA*

*Matthew Johnson*
*Canadian Region Director*

*Referring piece: This is an internal and private document written by Matthew Johnson. No one has been given permission to post, copy, edit the report/article in parts or in whole. We ask that you work in accordance with DMCA take-down procedures to remove the copyrighted piece from the link above.*

*Sincerely,*
*Kathryn Baker, Operations Manager - SFWA*

SFWA's attempt to bury it notwithstanding, you can read considerably more about the report and my detailed response to it at HTTP://VOXDAY.BLOGSPOT.COM/2014/08/THE-RESPONSE.HTML if you wish. To this day, SFWA has neither publicly nor privately asserted that I was actually expelled from the organization, only that the SFWA Board voted unanimously for my expulsion. And while it is true that the SFWA Board vote took place, the fact is that no membership vote on the matter ever did, as required by the Massachusetts state law, specifically, Part I, Title XXII, Chapter 180, Section 18.

> *No member of such corporation shall be expelled by vote of less than a majority of all the members thereof, nor by vote of less than three quarters of the members present and voting upon such expulsion.*

In any event, those are the simple facts of the matter. SJWs always lie. I don't.

# Books by Vox Day

## Non-Fiction
*SJWs Always Lie: Taking Down the Thought Police*
*The Irrational Atheist: Dissecting the Unholy Trinity of Dawkins, Harris, and Hitchens*
*The Return of the Great Depression*
*Riding the Red Horse* ed. with LTC Tom Kratman

## Fantasy
*A Magic Broken*
*A Throne of Bones, Arts of Dark and Light Book One*
*A Sea of Skulls, Arts of Dark and Light Book Two* (2016)
*The Wardog's Coin*
*The Last Witchking*
*Summa Elvetica: A Casuistry of the Elvish Controversy*
*The Altar of Hate*
*The War in Heaven*
*The World in Shadow*
*The Wrath of Angels*

## Science Fiction
*QUANTUM MORTIS A Man Disrupted* by Steve Rzasa and Vox Day
*QUANTUM MORTIS Gravity Kills* by Steve Rzasa and Vox Day
*QUANTUM MORTIS A Mind Programmed* by Jeff Sutton, Jean Sutton, and Vox Day
*Rebel Moon* by Bruce Bethke, and Vox Day